GLOBALISM

OR

NATIONALISM

HILLARY'S GLOBALISM OR TRUMP'S AMERICA

By

Kimberly Bratton

Vixen Publishing

Printed in the United States of America
First Printing, 2016
ISBN-13: 978-1537224947
ISBN-10:1537224948

Vixen Publishing

Contact Information
Vixen Publishing   www.vixenpublishing.com
Email us at: kimberlybratton@vixenpublishing.com

Some research material came from Wikipedia and is released under the
Creative Commons Attribution-Share-Alike License 3.0
http://creativecommons.org/licenses/by-sa/3.0/
Wikipedia® is a registered trademark of the Wikimedia Foundation, Inc., a
non-profit organization.

"Where globalization means, as it so often does, that the rich and powerful now have new means to further enrich and empower themselves at the cost of the poorer and weaker, we have a responsibility to protest in the name of universal freedom."

Nelson Mandela

KIMBERLY BRATTON

DEDICATION

I would like to dedicate this book to America, the land of the free and to all of her loving and generous people. It is because of them that America continues on fighting the battles that try to squash us every day. As patriotic Americans we are proud, stubborn and we will never allow our country to fall to those who wish to do her harm. America is the best country on the planet and there are so many who will be crushed to see her fall. We will not let that happen. To Patriots everywhere, stand up and fight. America needs you and we need America.

Thank you for reading,

Kimberly Bratton

KIMBERLY BRATTON

A NOTE TO THE READER

Dear Reader,

I want to thank you for reading my book on Hillary's Globalism - Trump's America. When I started writing this book, I had no idea what I was getting into. The things I found out through research have made me ill as I have realized just how badly the globalist want to destroy the American spirit. Their plans are worse than you can imagine. I believe I can truly say that this is one book that I wish I had never written because I would rather not know all the things I now know.

After months of research, I came to the conclusion that globalism is not what I want for my country as it will replace everything American hold sacred, like freedom and sovereignty.

Hillary Clinton is not a friend to any American citizen. Instead, she prefers illegals and Muslims to the people of America.

She has made it clear that her intentions are not in line with who we are as Americans.

Donald Trump, on the other hand, has made me proud to be an American. He reminds us that all we have to do is believe in America and in him and together, as a team, we will Make America Great Again.

I sincerely hope you enjoy reading the book and I believe you will come away from your reading with a full understanding of what Globalism is, where it came from, where it is going and who is involved in its implementation.

If after reading it you have a few minutes, I would greatly appreciate if you would write a short review on your experience on Amazon and/or Smashwords.

Thank you again,

Kimberly Bratton

THE BILL OF RIGHTS – FULL TEXT

Amendment I

Congress shall make no law respecting an establishment of religion, or prohibiting the free exercise thereof; or abridging the freedom of speech, or of the press; or the right of the people peaceably to assemble, and to petition the government for a redress of grievances.

Amendment II

A well regulated militia, being necessary to the security of a free state, the right of the people to keep and bear arms, shall not be infringed.

Amendment III

No soldier shall, in time of peace be quartered in any house, without the consent of the owner, nor in time of war, but in a manner to be prescribed by law.

Amendment IV

The right of the people to be secure in their persons, houses, papers, and effects, against unreasonable searches and seizures, shall not be violated, and no warrants shall issue, but upon probable cause, supported by oath or affirmation, and particularly describing the place to be searched, and the persons or things to be seized.

Amendment V

No person shall be held to answer for a capital, or otherwise infamous crime, unless on a presentment or indictment of a grand jury, except in cases arising in the land or naval forces, or in the militia, when in actual service in time of war or public danger; nor shall any person be subject for the same offense to be twice put in jeopardy of life or limb; nor shall be compelled in any criminal case to be a witness against himself, nor be deprived of life, liberty, or property, without due process of law; nor shall private property be taken for public use, without just compensation.

Amendment VI

In all criminal prosecutions, the accused shall enjoy the right to a speedy and public trial, by an impartial jury of the state and district wherein the crime shall have been committed, which district shall have been previously ascertained by law, and to be informed of the nature and cause of the accusation; to be confronted with the witnesses against him; to have compulsory process for obtaining witnesses in his favor, and to have the assistance of counsel for his defense.

Amendment VII

In suits at common law, where the value in controversy shall exceed twenty dollars, the right of trial by jury shall be preserved, and no fact tried by a jury, shall be otherwise reexamined in any court of the United States, than according to the rules of the common law.

Amendment VIII

Excessive bail shall not be required, nor excessive fines imposed, nor cruel and unusual punishments inflicted.

Amendment IX

The enumeration in the Constitution, of certain rights, shall not be construed to deny or disparage others retained by the people.

Amendment X

The powers not delegated to the United States by the Constitution, nor prohibited by it to the states, are reserved to the states respectively, or to the people

Table of Contents

INTRODUCTION

Donald Trump announced his run for the presidency one year ago, on June 16, 2015 and it was a day that brought hope to Americans around the country once again.

Far too many citizens have given up on our nation's future, as Barack Obama continues on his destructive path of "fundamentally transforming" our country into something most of us no longer recognize. From his devastatingly expensive Affordable Healthcare Act, to his sovereignty dissolving trade agreements, most Americans see their future as bleak and scary. President Obama has brought in nearly one million Muslims in his tenure and plans to spend his last month's peppering our nation with millions more of them. With the Muslims and migrants the administration is bringing in also comes diseases that have been eradicated here in America for decades.

Obama has proven to be the most divisive President in history, pitting every citizen and every ethnicity against each other, in his desire to tear the

United States apart. The most devastating fact is; he has been extremely successful in his efforts.

In my lifetime, I have never before seen such division and hate within this nation, hate that is collapsing families and friendships, as the politics become ever-more toxic. I have lost friends myself over Obama and now Hillary Clinton, as I fight for what I believe in and I fight for my children's futures. I have family members that I no longer want to be around because of their closed minds and inability to admit that they made a huge mistake in voting for Obama. I watch as their lives are flushed down the toilet, financially ruined, with no hope of ever recovering, but still, they cling to their ignorant and stubborn denial of the truth. Obama has ruined this country and it only took him 8 years to do it. It seems that Obama's transformation of America means taking it backwards.

Hillary Clinton will continue with the Obama agenda and she minces no words about it. She is a devout Globalist, who subscribes to The New World Order and her plans for this nation are even scarier and more devastating than Obama's have been.

Clinton will remove what is left of our borders and will flood our nation with as many as four million more Muslims before her first term is up, and she will surrender our country to the United Nations and the Globalist agenda. She will completely disarm Americans, leaving us defenseless in the wake of Radical Islamic Terrorism and we will no longer be able to protect our families from the ever growing violence that has infiltrated our once peaceful society.

Barack Obama has allowed our law enforcement officers to be taunted and murdered by a domestic terrorist group called Black Lives Matters (BLM). This group, with the help of Obama, Hillary Clinton, and a monster named George Soros, have brought terror and death to cities all over the nation. They march in groups, brandishing weapons, side by side with the New Black Panthers, all funded by George Soros, while chanting "death to the pigs" and "death to whitey." They were once considered insignificant, but the Obama administration has encouraged them, funded them and allowed them to get away with heinous hate crimes and murder.

George Soros is a well known supporter of American progressive and liberal political causes.

Between 1979 and 2011, Soros donated more than $11 billion, funding more than 170 organizations whose purpose is wreck havoc on the world as a whole. Soros is a well known and hated man who lives only to see the destruction of America and the rise of Globalism.

Barack Obama and Hillary Clinton are two of the most dangerous people on the planet. They must be stopped at any cost if we want to have a nation with a Constitution that protects our freedoms. There is only one man who is willing to take on this challenge. One man who is capable of reversing this ship we call the Titanic before it sinks once and for all.

That man is Donald Trump and I will make it known here that I support him completely and will be casting my vote for him because I believe he will be able to save the future for my children and grand children. I have never been one to trust people easily, but over the past year, I have come to realize that I can and do trust Donald J. Trump.

I have watched almost every rally he has done this past year and if he is nothing else, he is consistent. He is not always eloquent in his delivery but he speaks from his heart, not from a teleprompter delivering a speech someone else has written. He doesn't lie, he is a straight-shooter and I for one, will be placing my trust and faith in him. He has won my heart but not just mine. He has won the heart of the nation and they too, most of them anyway, are willing to stand tall, proud, and announce their allegiance to him.

We all want the same thing, we want our country back. We want to have a future filled with hope, dreams and the freedoms provided for us in our Constitution. If Clinton becomes the next president, our Constitution will become null and void as she will destroy what Obama has left of it, tearing it to pieces and we will no longer be a free society. We simply can't allow this to happen.

This election is THE election of our life-time and we must fight like we have never fought before. We must elect Donald Trump or our beloved country, the United States of America, will exist no more.

My first political book, "Donald Trump: An American Love-Fest" turned out to be an easy book to write and a fun-filled book to read. It chronicles Donald Trump supporters, who they are, and what they are feeling about the untested candidate who stole the hearts of so many. It was great to get to know each and every one of his supporters and they loved telling the world why they are willing to take a chance on the billionaire businessman turned politician. They are amazing people and I thank them all for their participation, because without them we would not be where we are today.

We have witnessed Donald Trump's support grow to unheard of levels. For an outsider candidate to do what this man has done is beyond amazing; it is truly spectacular.

Each day brings new revelations about the state of our country and the world. We live in dangerous times, growing more so every day. While other politicians are afraid to talk about the issues, Donald Trump is not afraid to bring them out into the open. He speaks honestly, not always politically correct, but correct nonetheless. That is what Trump supporters love most about him. He tells us the truth, as bad as it can be sometimes, but the truth is what we need to hear after so many years of ambiguity.

My second politically motivated book, "Donald Trump: The People's Choice" tells the story of a remarkable man who has fought a fierce battle to the top and has remained there for months. Donald Trump has had to fight the political machine and the status quo, but he has made it this far and will continue to fight for America. Donald Trump will never stop because he believes in all of us. He loves our country more than himself and he proves it every day. He lives an amazing life, full of love, hope, and riches and he simply wants the same for all of us.

We began this journey with seventeen candidates, amazing individuals, who worked tirelessly competing in one of the most grueling primaries in history. They all fought the good fight, but only one will move to the finish line.

The final chapter of "The People's Choice" travels beyond the United States, as World Leaders weigh in on the American election. A great deal of them support the Democrat challenger, Hillary Clinton and by the time you finish reading this book, you will understand why they support her and why it is so important that we defeat her. We will explore what Hillary Clinton, the Globalist, has in store for our nation, should she become the next President and I promise you, it will not be pleasant for any of us.

These books I have written are dedicated to all the patriots who fought for and voted for our 2016 GOP Presidential nominee, Donald Trump. It is their love for America that drove so many to participate in this election.

Future generations will one day thank us for everything we worked for and how hard we fought. It is because of them, our children and grand-children, that we did this, together, to elect a man whose only desire is make a better life for everyone.

We have no more time for fighting amongst ourselves, we must come together, unify behind Donald Trump, because if we don't, none of us will be safe, and America will be lost. It is crunch time, so make your vote count because if you don't, this may be the last vote you ever cast.

This book is centered around Hillary Clinton's vision for a Globalist world, controlled by the elites, those wealthy people who plan to control every aspect of people's lives, versus Donald Trump's vision of America First, while ensuring the safety and prosperity of the rest of the world at the same time.

This book will follow what has promised to be an extremely nasty campaign as Donald Trump and Hillary Clinton square off. It will be interesting and terrifying and hopefully, when it is all over, the best man will be standing. Hopefully, we will have a President Donald J. Trump.

Good Luck to us all but most importantly, Good Luck to America.

Kimberly Bratton

PART 1

GLOBALISM

AND

HILLARY CLINTON

"We must ensure that the global market is embedded in broadly shared values and practices that reflect global social needs, and that all the world's people share the benefits of globalization."
Kofi Annan

KIMBERLY BRATTON

SOMETHING TO THINK ABOUT

Democrats continue to say that they are the champions of the poor/middle class while they rail on about how the system is rigged in favor of the millionaires, billionaires, big business, etc.

Is it not Democrats themselves who are in fact rigging the system on behalf of these millionaires, billionaires, big business, etc. by providing them with the cheap labor they seek in direct competition with & to the detriment of our own citizens, especially the poor/middle class thus enabling the rich to enrich themselves even further??? (Why do you suppose that Wall Street and Silicon Valley gives so much money to Democrats.)

Democrats greedy for power desperately want an expanded voter base paid for by the American people/taxpayers and apparently have no problem w/Americans being replaced w/cheap labor and having their wages reduced while being forced to also subsidize this cheap labor. How can Democrats possibly claim to be the champions of the poor/middle class while simultaneously serving as the instrument of their destruction?

Democrats who advocate for citizenship for millions of illegals and their families & seek open borders. The very people who are responsible for lost jobs and reduced wages for American citizens????

Democrats who constantly speak about the unfairness of the separation of illegal alien families & seek to reunite them here in the US at the expense of the American people/taxpayers???

Democrats who fight so hard to provide them with taxpayer funded benefits and even seek to normalize their presence and make their lives easier and more convenient here in the US by providing them with driver's licenses???

Democrats who seek to include them in Obamacare and even provide them with taxpayer funded subsidies while our own vets lack the care they need?

Democrats who even now are fighting to give them the right to vote here in the US even though they are here illegally. They are citizens of other nations and yet Democrats would give them the power to set the laws in our nation that would benefit them???

Democrats need to clarify who they are truly the champions of because it is they who are pitting our own citizens against those of other nations. They are forcing our citizens to compete in a competition that is clearly stacked against them, a competition they cannot win.

1. Median Household Income in Jan 2009 was around $56,957, in Nov 2015 $56,746. Completely flatten out and hasn't recovered under Obama.

2. Labor Participation Rate in Jan 2009 was 65%, in Nov 2015 62.6% under Obama which is a 40 year low.

3. Americans on Food Stamps in Jan 2009 was 31.9 million, Nov 2015 it has risen to 45.8 million. A 42% growth, not the type of growth any healthy economy wants, and it's still rising under Obama. Food Stamps for Blacks have risen 58%, that's nothing to be proud about.

4. American Poverty Rates under Obama grew from 39.9 million in 2008 to 46.7 million in 2014, a 17% increase. Obama create MORE POOR PEOPLE which most were Black and Women.....GET IT!

5. The U.S. National Debt in Jan 2009 was 10.62 Trillion $, in 2016 it is 18.9 Trillion and

climbing, up 77% under the Uber President which is more than all Presidents combine.....all of them. Oh yea, our crediting rating went down too.

6. Thirty percent (30%) of Likely U.S. Voters think the country is heading in the right direction, only 30%, which includes democrats of course. This means Voters think the Nation is going in the WRONG direction....WRONG direction which of course Crooked Hillary would stay the course.

7. Now for my master 'coup de grace' Race Relations. 34% of Americans say it's good while 64% say it's bad. Obama was suppose to bring Americans together is a spirit of Kumbaya but instead managed to divide US like no other President in the Modern Era for the sole purpose of advancing Socialism. When Obama speaks about 'A more Perfect Union' he means making the Nation more Socialist, not FREE!

"The United Nations remains our most important global actor. These days we are continuously reminded of the enormous responsibility of the Security Council to uphold international peace and stability."

Anna Lindh

CHAPTER 1

THE UNITED NATIONS

This book will describe Nationalism and Globalism; but in order to fully understand exactly what they are and how they came to be, we must understand a little about the history of each, so we will start with the creation of the United Nations.

In the 21st century, the United Nations (UN) remains an intergovernmental organization created for the purpose of promoting international co-operation and security in the aftermath of World War II. Its main objective being the prevention of another devastating war. At its initial creation, the UN boasted 51 member states; that number has now grown to 193.

Headquarters located in Manhattan, Geneva, Nairobi, Hague, and Vienna, are financed by member states. Its objectives include maintaining international peace and security, preserving human rights, promoting social and economic development, protecting the environment, and providing humanitarian aid in cases of famine, natural disaster, and armed conflict.

The official United Nations Charter was drafted between April and June of 1945, and once completed, it went into effect on October 24, 1945. Now the UN could begin its peacekeeping operations.

Today, the UN has six principal organs and I will explain their individual responsibilities a little later in this chapter.

1. The General Assembly.
2. The Security Council.
3. The Economic and Social Council.
4. The Secretariat.
5. The International Court of Justice.
6. The United Nations Trusteeship Council (inactive since 1994).

Four of the five principal organs are located at the main UN Headquarters in New York City. The International Court of Justice is located in Hague, while the remaining agencies are based in the UN offices at Geneva, Vienna, and Nairobi. While still other UN institutions are located throughout the world.

The six official languages of the United Nations, used in intergovernmental meetings and documents, are Arabic, Chinese, English, French,

Russian, and Spanish. Based on the Convention on the Privileges and Immunities of the United Nations, the UN and all of its agencies are immune from the laws of the countries where they operate, ostensibly to safeguard the UN's impartiality with regard to the host and member countries.

Other agencies assisting the UN were the World Bank Group, the World Health Organization, the World Food Programs, UNESCO, and UNICEF.

The UN's most prominent officer is the Secretary-General, an office held by South Korean Ban Ki-moon since 2007. Non-governmental organizations may also be granted consultative status to assist in the UN's agenda.

While the organization won the Nobel Peace Prize in 2001, and a number of its officers and agencies have also been awarded the prize, other evaluations of the UN's effectiveness have been mixed. Some believe the organization to be an important force for peace and human development, while others have called the organization ineffective, corrupt, or biased.

In 2016, the United Nations has become an organization that most people fear, as they have become extremely powerful. Under the guise of

Globalism and the New World Order, the UN is seen as an organization who has the ability to take over nations and dictate to the world what they expect to see within those nations. With the cooperation of a certain group of world leaders, Barack Obama being just one of them, the UN is attempting to take over the sovereignty of every nation in the World.

In order to stop this, the people must make a choice. That choice is clear, do we allow Globalism or do we take our countries back and demand Nationalism. We will explore the differences in great detail.

The History of the United Nations:

In the century prior to the creation of the UN, several international treaty organizations and conferences had been formed to regulate conflicts between nations, such as the International Committee of the Red Cross and the Hague Conventions of 1899 and 1907.

With the devastating loss of life in World War I, the Paris Peace Conference established the "League of Nations" whose purpose was to maintain harmony between countries. The League would resolve some territorial disputes but mainly they created international structures such as postal mail, aviation, and control of opium production. The League, being poorly backed, failed in its representation of more than half the world's population (colonial people). Without participation from several major powers, including the US, USSR, Germany, and Japan; the League failed to act against the 1931 Japanese invasion of Manchuria, the 1935 Second Italo-Ethiopian War, the 1937 Japanese invasion of China, and the German expansions under Adolf Hitler that culminated with World War II. These failures would eventually be the downfall of The League of Nations.

Once it became apparent that the League of Nations would not be capable of living up to the expectations of its creators, a new world organization plan was formulated. This new organization was endorsement of the US State Department in 1939, and by 1942 the "Declaration by United Nations" was solidified as the plan for a new world organization.

The text of the "Declaration by United Nations" was drafted by President Franklin Roosevelt, British Prime Minister Winston Churchill, and Roosevelt aide Harry Hopkins, during a meeting at the White House on December 29, 1941. It incorporated Soviet suggestions, but left no role for France.

The phrase, "Four Policemen" was then coined to refer to the four major allied countries, United States, United Kingdom, Soviet Union, and China.

Roosevelt later conceived the term United Nations to describe the four allied countries and Churchill accepted this new terminology. On New Year's Day 1942, President Roosevelt, Prime Minister Churchill, Maxim Litvinov, of the USSR, and T. V. Soong, of China, would all sign a first draft document that became known as the United Nations Declaration. The following day the representatives of twenty-two other nations added their signatures to the document.

This new Declaration, as known as the Joint Declaration, consisted of: The United States Of America, The United Kingdom Of Great Britain And Northern Ireland, The Union Of Soviet Socialist Republics, China, Australia, Belgium, Canada, Costa Rica, Cuba, Czechoslovakia, Dominican Republic, El Salvador, Greece, Guatemala, Haiti, Honduras, India, Luxembourg,

Netherlands, New Zealand, Nicaragua, Norway, Panama, Poland, South Africa, and Yugoslavia.

The President of the United States and the Prime Minister of Great Britain, having agreed upon the common program of purposes and principles embodied in the Joint Declaration, established what became known as the Atlantic Charter and was dated, August 14, 1941.

The two leaders were convinced that complete victory over their enemies was essential to defend life, liberty, independence and freedom of religion. Preserving human rights and justice in their own lands, as well as in other lands, was also necessary for peace. By joining efforts they were now engaged in a common struggle against savage and brutal forces seeking to subjugate the world.

The U.S. and Great Britain agreed upon the following pledges to each other and the world:

(1) Each Government would pledge to employ its full resources, military or economic, against members of the Tripartite Pact and its adherents with which such a government is at war.

The Tripartite Pact, also known as the Berlin Pact, was an agreement between Germany, Italy and Japan, signed in Berlin on September 27, 1940 by, respectively, Joachim von Ribbentrop, Galeazzo Ciano and Saburō Kurusu. This pact was primarily directed at the U.S. but could be used to wage war on any nation they decided upon. Albeit, the pact had limitations, such as distance between cooperating nations, the U.S. and Great Britain took them seriously anyway.

(2) Each Government pledges itself to cooperate with the Governments signatory hereto and not to make a separate armistice or peace with the enemies.

The foregoing declaration may be adhered to by other nations which are, or which may be, rendering material assistance and contributions in the struggle for victory over Hitlerism.

During a war, the United Nations would become the official term for the Allies. To join, countries had to sign the Declaration and be ready to declare war, if necessary.

The first official meetings of the United Nations General Assembly, with 51 nations represented, and the Security Council took place in London on January 6, 1946. The Norwegian

Foreign Minister, Trygve Lie, was elected as the first UN Secretary-General and the UN then commenced to begin its intended purpose.

In 1947, the General Assembly approved a resolution to partition Palestine, approving the creation of the state of Israel. Two years later, Ralph Bunche, a UN official, would negotiate an armistice to the resulting conflict.

Even though the UN's primary mandate was peacekeeping, it was often paralyzed during the Cold War era, with the division between the US and USSR. It was generally allowed to intervene only in conflicts distant from the Cold War. An exception to this, passed without input from the USSR, was a Security Council resolution in 1950 which authorized a US-led coalition to repel the North Korean invasion of South Korea.

In 1956, the UN peacekeeping force was commandeered to end the Suez Crisis; however, it was unable to intervene against the USSR's simultaneous invasion of Hungary following that country's revolution.

In 1960, the UN deployed Operations in the Congo, the largest military force used to date, to bring order to the breakaway State of Katanga. It was restored to the control of the Democratic Republic of the Congo in 1964.

With the spread of decolonization in the 1960's, the organization's membership saw an influx of newly independent nations. In 1960 alone, 17 new states joined the UN, 16 of them from Africa. By the 70's its budget for economic and social development programs far outpaced its spending on peacekeeping.

With opposition from the United States, but with the support of many Third World nations, the communist People's Republic of China was granted the Chinese seat on the Security Council instead of the Republic of China which occupied Taiwan. This October 25, 1971 vote was widely seen as a sign of waning US influence in the organization.

Third World nations organized a "Group of 77" coalition under the leadership of Algeria. They would briefly become a dominant power at the UN. In 1975, a bloc comprising the USSR and Third World nations passed a resolution, over strenuous US and Israeli opposition, declaring Zionism to be racism. This unwanted resolution was repealed in 1991, shortly after the end of the Cold War.

With the increase of the Third World presence and the failure of UN mediation in conflicts in the Middle East, Vietnam, and Kashmir, the UN shifted its attention to its secondary goals of economic development and cultural exchange. By the 1970's, the UN budget for social and economic development was far greater than its peacekeeping budget.

Between 1988 and 2000, the number of adopted Security Council resolutions would more than double, and the peacekeeping budget increased more than tenfold. The UN negotiated an end to the Salvadoran Civil War, launched a successful peacekeeping mission in Namibia, and oversaw democratic elections in post-apartheid South Africa and post-Khmer Rouge Cambodia.

Although the UN Charter had been written primarily to prevent aggression by one nation against another, by early 1990 the UN would face a mounting number of simultaneous, serious crises within the nations of Somalia, Haiti, Mozambique, and the former Yugoslavia.

The UN's mission in Somalia was considered a failure after the US withdrew following casualties in the Battle of Mogadishu, and the UN mission to Bosnia would face "worldwide scorn" for its indecisive and confused mission in the face of ethnic cleansing. In 1994, the United Nations Assistance Mission for Rwanda would also fail, amid indecision within the Security Council, to intervene in the Rwandan Genocide.

In the last decade of the Cold War, American and European critics of the UN would condemn the organization for perceived mismanagement and corruption.

In 1984, the US President, Ronald Reagan, withdrew his nation's funding from the United Nations Educational, Scientific and Cultural Organization, which had been founded in 1946, over allegations of mismanagement. This drastic step by the U.S. was then followed by Britain and Singapore.

Boutros-Ghali, Secretary-General from 1992 to 1996, would reform the Secretariat thus reducing the size of the organization to some degree. His successor, Kofi Annan (1997–2006), would initiated further management reforms due in part from threats made by the United States to withhold its UN dues.

In the late 1990's and early 2000's, the UN granted international interventions that took a variety of forms. The UN mission in the 1991–2002 Sierra Leone Civil War was supplemented by the British Royal Marines, and the invasion of Afghanistan in 2001 was overseen by NATO, the North Atlantic Treaty Organization.

In 2003, the United States invaded Iraq despite their failure to pass a UN Security Council resolution for authorization. This breach prompted a new round of questions with regard to the organization's actual effectiveness.

Under the current Secretary-General, Ban Ki-moon, the UN has intervened with peacekeepers in crises including the War in Darfur in Sudan and the Kivu conflict in the Democratic Republic of Congo. They also sent observers and chemical weapons inspectors to the Syrian Civil War. During the 2010 Haiti earthquake, one hundred and one UN personnel died resulting in the worst loss of life in the organization's history.

In 2013, an internal review of UN actions in the final battles of the 2009 Sri Lankan Civil War, concluded that the organization was suffering from "systemic failure".

The United Nations adheres to the Noblemaire principle of salary which is binding on any organization that belongs to the United

Nations system. This principal is used for the determination of salary of staff members. Under the principle, salaries of staff members are determined not by the country they are working for but by the country with the highest level of pay for that position. This principle calls for the guarantee of salaries insuring that members are paid the highest salaries possible, regardless of the staff members location and nationality. Staff salaries are subject to an internal tax that is administered by the UN organizations and not by the country of origin.

The specific responsibilities of the principals organs of the United Nations are as follows:

The most influential member of the UN is the Secretary General and is appointed by the General Assembly, for a five-year term, after being recommended by the Security Council, where the permanent members have veto power. There is no specific criteria for the post, but over the years it has become accepted that the post shall be appointed on the basis of geographical rotation, and that the Secretary General shall not originate from one of the five permanent Security Council member states.

The Secretary General acts as the de facto leader of the UN. The position is defined in the UN Charter as the organization's "chief administrative officer", and can bring to the Security Council's attention "any matter which in his opinion may threaten the maintenance of international peace and security". The office has evolved into a dual role of an administrator of the UN organization and a diplomat and mediator addressing disputes between member states and finding consensus to global issues.

The General Assembly is the main deliberative assembly of the United Nations and is comprised of all UN Members. The assembly meets in regular yearly sessions, but emergency sessions can also be called, as needed. The assembly is led by a president, elected from among the member states on a rotating regional basis, and 21 vice-presidents.

It is responsible for resolving non-compulsory recommendations to states or suggestions to the Security Council (UNSC). They decides on the admission of new members proposed by the UNSC. They adopt the budget and elects the non-permanent members of the UNSC; all members of ECOSOC; the UN Secretary

General (following his/her proposal by the UNSC) and the fifteen judges of the International Court of Justice (ICJ).

When the General Assembly votes on important issues, a two-thirds majority of those present and voting is required. Such issues would include election of members; including the admission, suspension, and expulsion of members, and budgetary matters. All other questions are decided by a majority vote. Each member country has one vote. Apart from approval of budgetary matters, resolutions are not binding on the members. The Assembly may make recommendations on any matters within the scope of the UN, except matters of peace and security that are under consideration by the Security Council.

The UN Security Council is responsible for the maintenance of international peace and security. They may also adopt compulsory resolutions. They are made up of a panel of fifteen judges who are elected by the UN General Assembly. There are fifteen members; five permanent members with veto power and ten elected members.

The Secretariat is the administrative organ which supports the other UN bodies. The Secretariat is headed by the Secretary-General while assisted by a staff of international civil servants worldwide. It provides studies, information, and facilities needed by United Nations bodies for their meetings. It also carries out tasks as directed by the Security Council, the General Assembly, the Economic and Social Council, and other UN bodies. It also provides for the organization of conferences, the writing of reports and the preparation of the budget.

The International Court of Justice (ICJ) is located in The Hague, in the Netherlands. It is the primary judicial organ of the UN. Established in 1945 by the UN Charter, the Court began work in 1946 as the successor to the Permanent Court of International Justice. The ICJ is comprised of fifteen judges each serving a 9-year term. They are appointed by the General Assembly and every sitting judge must be from a different nation.

The ICJ's primary purpose is to adjudicate disputes among states that recognize its jurisdiction and renders judgment by relative majority. The court has heard cases related to war crimes, illegal state interference, ethnic cleansing, and other issues. The ICJ can also be called upon by other UN organs to provide advisory opinions. It decides disputes between states

The UN Economic and Social Council is responsible for co-operation between states as regards economic and social matters. It coordinates cooperation between the UN's numerous specialized agencies. It has 54 members, elected by the General Assembly to serve staggered three-year terms.

The UN Trusteeship Council was originally designed to manage colonial possessions that were former League of Nations mandates. It has been inactive since 1994, when Palau, the last trust territory, attained independence.

The Economic and Social Council (ECOSOC) assists the General Assembly in promoting international economic and social cooperation and development. ECOSOC has 54 members, which are elected by the General Assembly for a three-year term. The president is elected for a one-year term, chosen from the small or middle powers which represent the ECOSOC. The council has one annual meeting in July which is held in either New York or Geneva. Being separate from the specialized bodies it coordinates, the ECOSOC's functions include information gathering, advising member nations, and making recommendations.

The ECOSOC's subsidiary bodies include the United Nations Permanent Forum on Indigenous Issues, which advises UN agencies on issues relating to indigenous peoples; The United Nations Forum on Forests, which co-ordinates and promotes sustainable forest management; The United Nations Statistical Commission, which co-ordinates information-gathering efforts between agencies; and the Commission on Sustainable Development, which co-ordinates efforts between UN agencies working toward sustainable development.

Draft resolutions can be forwarded to the General Assembly by eight committees:

General Committee – a supervisory committee consisting of the assembly's president, vice-president, and committee heads.

Credentials Committee – responsible for determining the credentials of each member nation's UN representatives.

First Committee (Disarmament and International Security).

Second Committee (Economic and Financial).

Third Committee (Social, Humanitarian, and Cultural).

Fourth Committee (Special Political and Decolonization).

Fifth Committee (Administrative and Budgetary).

Sixth Committee (Legal).

Security Council.

The UN Charter stipulates that each primary organ of the UN can establish various specialized agencies to fulfill its duties. Some best-known agencies are the International Atomic Energy Agency, the Food and Agriculture Organization, UNESCO (United Nations Educational, Scientific and Cultural Organization), the World Bank, and the World Health Organization (WHO). The UN performs most of its humanitarian work through these agencies, such as mass vaccination programs, the avoidance of famine and malnutrition, and the protection of vulnerable and displaced people.

Organizations and specialized agencies of the United Nations include the following:

Acronym	Agency
FAO	Food and Agriculture Organization
IAEA	International Atomic Energy Agency
ICAO	International Civil Aviation Org.
IFAD	International Fund for Agricultural
ILO	International Labour Organization
IMO	International Maritime Org.
IMF	International Monetary Fund
ITU	International Telecommunication Union
UNESC	UN Educational, Scientific and Cultural
UNIDO	United Nations Industrial Development
UNWTO	World Tourism Organization
UPU	Universal Postal Union
WBG	World Bank Group
WFP	World Food Program
WHO	World Health Organization
WIPO	World Intellectual Property Org.
WMO	World Meteorological Org.

Membership in the United Nations is open to all other peace-loving states that agree to the obligations contained in the present Charter and, in the judgment of the Organization, are able and willing to carry out these obligations.

The admission of any such state to membership in the United Nations will be effected by a decision of the General Assembly upon the recommendation of the Security Council.

In addition, there are two non-member observer states of the United Nations General Assembly: the Holy See (which holds sovereignty over Vatican City) and the State of Palestine. The Cook Islands and Niue, both states in free association with New Zealand, are full members of several UN specialized agencies and have had their "full treaty-making capacity" recognized by the Secretariat.

United Nations peacekeeping and List of United Nations peacekeeping missions include the following:

The UN, after approval by the Security Council, will send in peacekeepers to regions where armed conflict has recently ceased to enforce the terms of the peace agreements and subsequently to discourage the resurgence of hostilities. Since the UN does not maintain its own military, peacekeeping forces are voluntarily provided by member states and these soldiers are sometimes nicknamed "Blue Helmets" for their distinctive gear. In 1988, the peacekeeping force as a whole received a Nobel Peace Prize.

In 2013, the UN had peacekeeping soldiers deployed on 15 different missions. The largest was the United Nations Organization Stabilization Mission in the Democratic Republic of the Congo. This mission included 20,688 uniformed personnel. The smallest mission was the United Nations Military Observer Group in India and Pakistan which included only 42 uniformed personnel responsible for monitoring the ceasefire in Jammu and Kashmir. UN peacekeepers with the United Nations Truce Supervision Organization have been stationed in the Middle East since 1948 which is the longest-running active peacekeeping mission.

A study in 2005 by the RAND Corporation, found the UN to be successful in two out of three peacekeeping efforts. The study compared efforts at nation-building by the UN to those of the U.S., and found that seven out of eight UN cases are at peace, while only four out of eight U.S. cases were at peace. Also in 2005, the Human Security Report documented a decline in the number of wars, genocides, and human rights abuses since the end of the Cold War. They presented evidence, albeit circumstantial, that international involvement, mostly spearheaded by the UN, was the main cause of the decline in armed conflict during that period.

The UN has also drawn criticism for perceived failures. In some cases, member states have shown a reluctance to enforce Security Council resolutions. These disagreements in regard to military action and intervention are seen as having failed to prevent the Bangladeshi genocide of 1971, the Cambodian genocide in the 70's, and the Rwandan genocide in 1994.

Additionally, the UN's lack of action is blamed for failing to prevent the Srebrenica massacre in 1995 and also for not completing its peacekeeping operations in 1992–93 during the Somali Civil War.

UN peacekeepers have also been accused of soliciting prostitution, participating in child rape, and various other sexual abuses during various peacekeeping missions in the Democratic Republic of the Congo, Haiti, Liberia, Sudan and what is now South Sudan, Burundi, and the Ivory Coast.

Scientists have also cited UN peacekeepers from Nepal as the likely source of the 2010–13 Haiti cholera outbreak, which killed more than 8,000 Haitians following the 2010 Haiti earthquake.

In addition to peacekeeping, failed or otherwise, the UN is active in encouraging disarmament. Regulation of armaments, included in the UN Charter of 1945, was considered a way of limiting the use of human and economic resources for the creation of arms. The advent of nuclear weapons came only weeks after the signing of the charter which resulted in the first resolution of the first General Assembly meeting. It called for the elimination of atomic weapons from national armaments and all other weapons which were adaptable to mass destruction. Some of the arms-limitation treaties in which the UN has been involved are; the Outer Space Treaty (1967), the Treaty on the Non-Proliferation of Nuclear Weapons (1968), the Seabed Arms Control Treaty (1971), the Biological Weapons Convention (1972), the Chemical Weapons Convention (1992), and the Ottawa Treaty (1997), which prohibits land-mines. The International Atomic Energy Agency, the Organization for the Prohibition of Chemical Weapons, and the Comprehensive Nuclear-Test-Ban Treaty Organization Preparatory Commission are the three UN bodies which currently oversee arms proliferation issues.

One of the UN's primary purposes is the promotion and encouragement for respect of human rights and for fundamental freedoms for all without distinction as to race, sex, language, or religion", and all members must pledge to undertake "joint and/or separate action" in order to protect these rights.

In 1948, the General Assembly adopted a Universal Declaration of Human Rights, drafted by Eleanor Roosevelt. It proclaims basic civil, political, and economic rights common to all human beings. The Declaration serves as a "common standard of achievement for all peoples and all nations" and has become the basis of two treaties, the 1966 International Covenant on Civil and Political Rights and the International Covenant on Economic, Social and Cultural Rights. In theory, the UN is not allowed to take action against human rights abuses without a Security Council resolution, but it does substantiate the investigating and reporting of such abuses.

In 1979, the General Assembly adopted the Convention on the Elimination of All Forms of Discrimination against Women, followed by the Convention on the Rights of the Child in 1989.

The United Nations Commission on Human Rights was formed in 1993 which would oversee human rights issues for the UN, following the recommendation of that year's World Conference on Human Rights, but was described as "broad and vague", while having "meager" resources to carry it out. In 2006, it was replaced by a Human Rights Council consisting of 47 nations and that same year, the General Assembly passed a Declaration on the Rights of Indigenous Peoples, and in 2011 it passed its first resolution recognizing the rights of LGBT people.

Millennium Development Goals for the Economic development and humanitarian assistance included the following platform:

1. Eradicate extreme poverty and hunger.
2. Achieve universal primary education.

3. Promote gender equality and empower women.

4. Reduce child mortality.

5. Improve maternal health.

6. Combat HIV/AIDS, malaria, and other diseases.

7. Ensure environmental sustainability.

8. Develop a global partnership for development.

The UN Development Program (UNDP), an organization for grant-based technical assistance founded in 1945, is one of the leading bodies in the field of international development and also publishes the UN Human Development Index, a comparative measure ranking countries by poverty, literacy, education, life expectancy, and other factors.

The Food and Agriculture Organization (FAO), was founded in 1945 and promotes agricultural development and food security.

UNICEF (the United Nations Children's Fund) was created in 1946 to aid European children after World War II and has since expanded its mission to provide aid around the world and to uphold the Convention on the Rights of the Child.

The World Bank Group and International Monetary Fund (IMF) are independent, specialized agencies and observers within the UN framework, according to a 1947 agreement. They were initially formed separately from the UN through the Bretton Woods Agreement in 1944. The World Bank provides loans for international development, while the IMF promotes international economic co-operation and gives emergency loans to indebted countries.

The World Health Organization (WHO) focuses on international health issues and disease eradication. It is one of the UN's largest agencies. In 1980, the agency announced that the eradication of smallpox had been completed. In subsequent decades, WHO largely eradicated polio, river blindness, and leprosy. The Joint United Nations Program on HIV/AIDS (UNAIDS) was created in 1996 and coordinates the response to the AIDS epidemic. The UN Population Fund also dedicates part of its resources to combating HIV and is the world's largest source of funding for reproductive health and family planning services.

Along with the International Red Cross and Red Crescent Movement, the UN often takes a leading role in coordinating emergency relief. In 1961, the World Food Program (WFP) was created to provide food aid in response to famine, natural disasters, and armed conflict. Reports indicate that the organization feeds an average of 90 million people in 80 nations every year.

Established in 1950, the Office of the United Nations High Commissioner for Refugees (UNHCR), works diligently to protect the rights of refugees and asylum seekers. The UNHCR and WFP programs are funded by voluntary contributions from governments, corporations, and individuals; however, administrative costs of the UNHCR are paid for by the UN's primary budget.

With the formation of the UN Environmental Program (UNEP) in 1972, environmental issues have become a prominent part of the UN's agenda. The 1992 Earth Summit in Rio de Janeiro, Brazil, sought to give new focus on these efforts, which had failed to catch on in the first two decades of the UNEP's existence. In 1988, UNEP and another UN organization know as the World Meteorological Organization (WMO), established the Intergovernmental Panel on

Climate Change. Their job is to assess and report on research on global warming, a concept that most people do not hold dear.

The UN is financed by the assessed contributions from member states. The General Assembly approves the budget and determines each members assessment or membership dues, if you will. This is based primarily on the relative capacity of each country to pay, as measured by its gross national income (GNI), making necessary adjustments for external debt and low per capita income, meaning the larger nations pay the majority of the membership fees. The two-year budget for 2012–13 was $5.512 billion dollars in total.

The General Assembly has established that the UN should not be dependent on any one member to finance its operations. Thus, a maximum rate paid by any member was then assessed. In December 2000, the Assembly revised the assessment scale in response to pressure from the United States. As part of that revision, the regular budget maximum was reduced from 25% to 22%. For lesser developed countries (LDCs), the maximum rate of 0.01% was applied. In addition , a minimum amount assessed to any member nation (or "floor" rate) is set at 0.001% of the UN budget or $55,120 for the two year budget 2013-2014.

The UN's largest expenditure addresses its core mission of peace and security, and this budget is assessed separately from the main administrative budget. The peacekeeping budget for the 2015–16 fiscal year was $8.27 billion and supports 82,318 troops deployed in 15 missions around the world. UN peace operations are funded by assessments, with the majority of those funds be derived from the five permanent Security Council members and must approve all peacekeeping operations. This scale of funds will offset discounted peacekeeping assessment rates for less developed countries.

In 2013, the top 10 providers of assessed financial contributions to United Nations peacekeeping operations were the United States (28.38%), Japan (10.83%), France (7.22%), Germany (7.14%), the United Kingdom (6.68%), China (6.64%), Italy (4.45%), the Russian Federation (3.15%), Canada (2.98%), and Spain (2.97%).

Since its conception, there have been many calls for reform of the United Nations. Some want the UN to play a greater role in world affairs, while others want its role reduced to only humanitarian work. The discrepancy in views depends primarily on whether or not you live in a developed nation or a developing nation, with the former wanting a lesser role for the UN while the latter wants a larger role.

Critics of the UN have accused it of bureaucratic inefficiency, waste, and corruption. In 1976, the General Assembly established the Joint Inspection Unit to determine where these inefficiencies were and to document ways to fix them. During the 1990's, the U.S. actually withheld membership dues citing inefficiency and corruption, and only started repayment on the condition that major reforms were introduced. This lead to the 1994 creation of the Office of Internal Oversight Services (OIOS) which would serve as an efficiency watchdog.

In 2004, the UN faced accusations that its recently ended Oil-for-Food Program, in which Iraq had been allowed to trade oil for basic needs to relieve the pressure of sanctions, had suffered from widespread corruption, including billions of dollars in kickbacks. An independent performed by the UN found that many of its officials had been involved, raising "significant" questions about the credibility of the entire organization.

It is believed by many that the UN as a whole has accomplished great things in the last 60 years, such as progress in human development during the 20th century and helping the world become a more hospitable place to live for millions. Others, however, believe that the United Nations never fulfilled the hopes of its founders, eventually became a self-serving organization. The British historian Paul Kennedy states that while the organization has suffered major setbacks, "when all its aspects are considered, the UN has brought great benefits to our generation and ... will bring benefits to our children's and grand-children's generations as well."

Whereas I believe in the altruistic intentions of the United Nations, I also believe that in 2016, it has indeed become a powerhouse of corruption and control. I believe that, while going against its grain, it is currently being used to serve a more devious agenda. An agenda that is not in the best interest of the world, but merely a few. It is becoming an instrument, used by the elites in their aspirations of Globalism and a New World Order.[1]

#

"During the boom years of the 1990's, globalization emerged as the most significant development in our national life. With NAFTA and the Internet and big-box stores selling cheap goods from China, the line between national and international began to blur."

Noah Feldman

CHAPTER 2

HISTORY OF GLOBALISM

Some people say Globalism is rooted in Communism, which is rooted in Marxism, and they would be correct as their ideological principals go hand in hand. To fully understand globalism, we must also understand the others.

In this chapter we will examine these ideologies and their relationship to one another. Below are the definitions of Globalism, Globalization, Marxism, Socialism, Communism, Democracy and Capitalism. Whereas some characteristics span the ideologies, there are distinct differences.

Globalism by definition is the attitude or policy of placing the interests of the entire world above those of individual nations. This one world order would then be controlled, for the purpose of political influence, by the elite or ruling class.

Globalization, not to be confused with Globalism, is a process of international interaction and integration among people, companies, and governments of different nations. This process is driven by international trade, global banking and investment, ease of travel and aided by information technology. The Internet, which made the world essentially a much smaller place, made Globalization an imminent process and has brought true Globalism closer than ever before.

Marxism is the political, economic, and social principles and policies advocated by Karl Marx. His ideology specifically relates to the theory and practice of socialism including the labor theory of value, dialectical materialism, the class struggle, and dictatorship of the proletariat class (working class or peasants) until the establishment of a classless society has been fully implemented and controlled by the ruling class.

Whereas we will not be discussing Socialism to a great extent, I want to add the true definition of Socialism here, for reference, mainly because Bernie Sanders is a self-proclaimed Socialist and today's Millennial believes Socialism is completely acceptable, that is until they are forced to actually live it.

Socialism is a political and economic theory of social organization. It is a way of organizing a society in which major industries are owned and controlled by the government rather than by individual people. It is characterized by social ownership and democratic control of all means of production whereby the individual owns nothing at all. It is all owned by and distributed by those in control, the elites. The idea is that all individuals must give according to their ability and receive according to their needs.

Communism is a social, political, and economic ideology and movement whose ultimate goal is the establishment of the communist society. The theory, derived from Karl Marx, is a socioeconomic order structured upon the common ownership of all means of production with the absence of social classes. Communism advocates class war, leading to a society in which all property is publicly owned and each person works and is paid according to their abilities and needs, very much like Socialism.

Democracy is a system of government in which all people of a state or organization are involved in making decisions about its affairs, typically by voting to elect representatives to certain positions of authority.

Capitalism is an economic system based on private ownership of all means of production and their operation for profit. In a capitalist society anyone who has the fortitude, intelligence and means to create, build and sell a brand could benefit monetarily, thus creating a better life for their family. There were no limitations, other than those self-imposed, to prevent anyone in a capitalist society from succeeding and a successful capitalist was able to own private property and obtain financial independence. Wage labor, voluntary exchange, a fair pricing through competitive markets were all characteristics of a successful capitalist society. In a capitalist economy, the decision-making and investment was determined by the individual owners and the pricing and distribution of goods are therefore determined mainly by consumers through competition within the markets.

In order to fully understand the principals of Globalism, we will delve a little deeper into the history of Marxism. Without Marxism, there cannot be Globalism.

Karl Marx, a German Ideologist, said in 1845 that "The ideas of the ruling class are the ruling ideas and that every lower social class would therefore be in servitude to the interests of the ruling class." Hence the idea that: "The *dominant ideology* is the ideology of the dominant class. This philosophy became known as Marxism.

The Ruling Class, by definition, is the social class of a given society that decides upon and sets society's political agenda by mandating that there is one such ruling class in a given society, and then appoints itself as that class. In the twenty-first century, the ruling class are commonly known as the "Elite Class" and most commonly believe in the Marxist version of the world and Globalism.

Dominant Ideology is defined by the attitudes and beliefs, values and morals shared by the elites or ruling class of modern day civilization. It is commonly used as a mechanism of social control, as it frames how the majority of the population behave regardless of circumstances, education, where you live or who you are.

In the 21st century, the most well know dominant class or Power Elites are Bill and Hillary Clinton, The Bush Family, President Barack Obama, The Mitt Romney Family, The Koch Brothers, George Soros, Michael Bloomberg, The Alice Walton Family (Wal-Mart Stores), Larry

Ellison, Warren Buffet, Bill Gates, Mark Zuckerberg, most Democrat and Republican politicians, including Paul Ryan and Mitch McConnell, the leaders of most every country, most celebrities, and the billionaires and millionaires of the world and their ilk. With the exception of a few, like Donald Trump, they all believe in Globalism, Marxism and the total control of the 99% of us who don't fall into their category of wealth. When reading about the Marxist Ideology, keep in mind the names of those I listed above as they believe that this philosophy is necessary for their survival but not necessarily yours.

What exactly is Marxist Ideology?

Simply put it is: Obtaining rule over the lower class of society by means of the ideological manipulation of every aspect of society through totalitarian control of religion and politics, economics and culture, in order to justify the political advantage and necessity of the dominant or ruling class. In modern Marxism, that also extends to personal security and the healthcare of the people. In the mind of the Marxist, such a method of social control is required for the stability of a Republic.

To completely understand Marxism, we must know the terminology with regards to "class of people". The Bourgeoisie is the working or middle class while the dominant class is essentially the ruling elites, such as those names I listed above.

The middle class was characterized by three different classes: the upper middle class (haute) referred to those with a certain cultural financial capital, whereas the lower middle class (petite) tended to be those who were small-scale merchants. The third group of middle class (moyenne) fell somewhere between the upper and lower classes.

The most affluent of the upper middle class were also known as the capitalist class and stood opposite the proletariat class or peasants; the poverty ridden "working class" who owned little or no property and whose only value was their ability to sell themselves as laborers. The proletariat class were considered the lowest class of society.

By the nineteenth century, Karl Marx would equate the ruling-class political system with the term dominant ideology, which described the societal status quo (religion, politics, economics, and culture) that characterized the capitalism of the nineteenth century. As such, the Marxist philosophy proposed two concepts of dominant ideology known as Intentional and Spontaneous.

Intentional ideology is deliberately constructed by the upper middle to middle class intellectuals of society, those who control the mass communications media; such as print, radio, television, cinema, and later, the Internet. Since this class generally owned the communications media, they could select and publish the economic, social, and cultural concepts that would most benefit their particular ideology. These hand-picked ideological publications would therefore serve only the interests of the ruling class of society.

Whereas, the proletariat class (the working class) were typically not able to own any form of mass communication and with the absence of any real intellectuals within their class to offer differing opinions, they were forced to accept the Intentional Ideology of the ruling classes as truth. The ruling class were therefore able to impose their worldview and economic exploitation upon the proletariat class. With that intentional exploitation, the working class lost their social and political, economic and cultural independence as a social class. To use phraseology we are most familiar with today; this Intentional Ideology meant that the elites of the world set the agenda for the rest, according to their elitist desires and whims. That is still happening today through the main stream media and liberal news outlets, such as ABC, CBS, NBC, CNN, FOX and MSNBC.

Spontaneous ideology emanates within all social classes of society. It is primarily based upon their experiences of societal life. Men and women of each social class would develop their own intellectual understanding of society based on their experiences. This type of ideology would allow for the masses to control the ideology instead of the elites. This shared ideology tended to reflect the norms of a capitalist society so therefore, the content of a newspaper was determined, not by the socio-economic and political prejudices of the elites, but instead by the society as a whole. Therefore, the social narrative was believed to be the status quo of society - the publisher and the readers of the newspaper.

Once workers began to organize as trade unions, the working class experienced a different type of social relation within a capitalist society. They began to challenge the intellectual and social legitimacy of capitalism, by questioning the validity of how society was organized, and how it should function. They established a successful working-class ideology which represented a collective approach to the socio-economic, political, and cultural problems of working-class people. Out of this new, rudimentary class consciousness within the capitalist society, sprang forth the ideology that expressed the interests of workers, and contradicted the status quo established by the dominant ideology of the ruling, elitist class.[2]

This new working class version of a capitalist society sought to render the ruling class as politically illegitimate, without power to dictate to the masses. With the absence of the ruling class, the working class would then be able to achieve and establish social, political, and economic dominance, giving them the ability to assume power, both politically and economically. They would then become the dominant class of the society and the ruling class was not about to let that happen.

Therefore, the ruling class decided that they must force global capitalism on the masses once and for all.

Paul James, Professor of Globalization and Cultural Diversity at Western Sydney University, defines globalism "as the *dominant ideology* and subjectivity associated with different historically-dominant formations of global extension. The definition thus implies that there were pre-modern or traditional forms of globalism and globalization long before capitalism became the driving force.

According to James, globalism can be traced back to the Roman Empire in the second century AD and perhaps to the Greeks of the fifth-century BC., so we can ascertain that the concept of globalism has been around for centuries.

The more modern evidence of globalization is the 19th century empire-building of England, Germany and Belgium in Africa. These empire building countries rushed to carve up Africa and plunder their natural and human resources. Globalization in Africa has been described as an "uneven process" due to the beneficial integration of some groups to the marginalization and exclusion of others. Tensions resulting from this were the cause of great conflict in the Niger Delta area.

Manfred Steger, Professor at the University of Hawaii at Manoa and until 2013 was Professor of Global Studies and Director of the Globalism Research Center at RMIT University in Australia, suggests that there are three distinctly different versions of globalism. They are justice globalism, religious or jihad globalism, and market globalism.

Justice globalism envisages a global civil society with fairer relationships and environmental safeguards. They disagree with market globalists who view neoliberalism as the only way. Religious globalism's strive for a global religious community with superiority over secular structures. This religious globalism is a view held primarily by Islam and Jihadis.

Market globalism advocates the promise of a consumerist, free-market world, characterized by networks of connections that span multi-continental distances consisting of many, if not all nations on the planet. This ideology is held by many powerful individuals, who claim it displaces democracy and benefits everyone. However, it also reinforces inequality as it is a class system controlled by the elites and is most often politically motivated.

The word itself, Globalism, came into widespread usage, first in the United States in the early 1940's. This was the period when U.S. global power was at its peak. The country was known as the greatest economic power the world had ever seen, having the greatest military in history. At that time the U.S. boasted to have about 50% of the world's wealth but only 6.3% of its population.

With this new and unprecedented power, the U.S. began to formulate policies that would shape the kind of world they wanted; which, in economic terms, meant a globe-spanning capitalist order centered exclusively upon the United States.

Capitalism was carried across the world by the broad processes of globalization and by the early 20th century, capitalism was adopted by most economies worldwide.

Industrialization, the extensive re-organization of an economy for the purpose of manufacturing, allowed cheap production of household items, using factors such as economies of scale, while rapid population growth created sustained demand for commodities. Globalization in this period was decisively shaped by 18th-century imperialism.

While global ideologies have a long history, true globalism emerged as the dominant ideology of the power elites throughout the course of the late 20th century. As these ideologies settled, and as various processes of globalization intensified, they contributed to the consolidation of a connected global consciousness, or a global community.

Globalist today ascertain that wealth inequality is the inevitable consequence in a capitalist economy and the resulting concentration of wealth can destabilize democratic societies and undermine the social justice upon which they were built.

Marxists, anarchists, and other leftists argue that capitalism is incompatible with democracy since capitalism according to Marx entails "dictatorship of the elites" while democracy entails rule by the people. This theory meant that capitalism and globalism were, therefore, primarily polar opposites of democracy.

Marx's theory is correct as capitalism leads to a significant loss of political, democratic and economic power for the vast majority of the global population. It creates very large concentrations of money and property in the hands of a relatively small group of the population, the Elite or the Power Elite. This downside to capitalism can lead to very large and increasing wealth and income inequalities between the elite and the majority of the population. For this reason, the rich keep getting richer while the working class keeps getting poorer.

To most people Globalism sounds like a beneficial prospect for the world, but the underlying fact is that it really only benefits the wealthiest and most influential members of the population. It is a merely a means to an end. It is their way of implementing their New World Order.[3]

"We are not going to
achieve a new world
order without paying
for it in blood as well as
in words and money."

Arthur Schlesinger,
Jr. 1995

CHAPTER 3

THE NEW WORLD ORDER

The term "New World Order" (NWO) has been used throughout time to refer to any period of history evidencing a new and dramatic change in world political thought and the balance of power.

In the 21st century, however, most people recognize it as being primarily associated with the ideological notion that it takes the collective efforts of a "global governance" to identify, understand, or address worldwide problems that go beyond the capacity of individual nations to resolve.

One of the earliest and most well-known Western uses of the term "new world order" was by Woodrow Wilson following the devastation of World War I, which had been justified not only in terms of U.S. national interest but in moral terms "to make the world safe for democracy."

The phrase "new world order" was explicitly used in connection with Wilson's global zeitgeist during the introduction phase of the League of Nations, which was a absolute failure and was later replaced by the United Nations, which we will discuss in the next chapter.

Wilson argued that a new world order would replace traditional power-politics by emphasizing collective security, democracy, and self-determination. "The war to end all wars" had been a powerful catalyst in international politics, and many felt that the world simply could not operate as it had been any longer.

The League of Nations was founded on January 10, 1920 and was an intergovernmental organization created out of the Paris Peace Conference which ended World War 1. The League was the first international organization whose principal mission was to maintain world peace. Its primary goals, as stated in its Covenant, were the prevention of future wars through collective security, disarmament and the settling of international disputes through negotiation and arbitration.

Other resolutions and treaties were then introduced to include labor conditions, just treatment of native inhabitants, human and drug trafficking, arms trade, global health, prisoners of war, and protection of minorities in Europe. By February of 1935, the League of Nations consisted of only 58 members.

The United States Senate rejected membership into the League of Nations, as Senator Henry Cabot Lodge argued that American policy should be based on human nature "as it is, not as it ought to be." With the absence of the powerful United States, the League was doomed to failure.

The League did fail as it was never able to complete most, if any, of the aforementioned resolutions. One important weakness grew from the contradiction between the idea of collective security that formed the basis of the League and international relations between individual states.

The League's collective security system required nations to act, if necessary, against states they considered friendly, which could endanger their national interests, but it also required these nations to protect and support other nations for which they had no real affinity. In all respects, most nations considered the Leagues collective security to be contradictory to the own best interest.

Countries were unwilling to disarm, out of fear of vulnerability, and as war after war broke out across the world, it became clear that the League was insufficient to complete its agenda. With no armed force of its own, it was forced to depend on the Great Powers to enforce its resolutions, but the two most important members, Britain and France, were reluctant to use sanctions and even more reluctant to resort to military action on behalf of the League.

The final meeting of the League of Nations took place on April 18, 1946 in Geneva. This final session concerned itself only with the liquidation of the League's assets. It transferred approximately $22,000,000 (U.S.) in assets, including the Palace of Peace and the League's archives to the United Nations, which was established in 1945. After settling all debts incurred by the League, it returned reserve funds to the nations that had supplied them, then the League of Nations was disbanded once and for all.

The phrase, new world order, was used again by Presidents Mikhail Gorbachev and George H. W. Bush while trying to define the nature of a post Cold War era, and the cooperation between the nations that they hoped might materialize.

At first, the new world order dealt almost exclusively with nuclear disarmament and security arrangements. Gorbachev would then expand the phrase to include UN strengthening and great power cooperation on a range of economic and security problems.

Mikhail Gorbachev's December 7, 1988 speech to the United Nations General Assembly, highlighted his vision for the creation of the new world order concept. He included an extensive list of ideas in creating a new order. He advocated strengthening the central role of the United Nations, and the active involvement of all members which would give the UN and its Security Council the ability to perform their roles as initially envisioned.

Gorbachev said that there must be a de-ideologizing of relations among states through which this new level of cooperation could be achieved. What Gorbachev meant by that was that the Soviet Union and the United States had to be prepared to accept political and social change, particularly in Eastern Europe, in order for there to be a peaceful existence for the entire world.

Gorbachev recognized what he perceived as the necessity of a one world economy, with the UN as the peacekeeper. He determined that with the cooperation of the superpowers, regional conflicts would no longer exist and that was especially key in his conception of cooperation. He argued that the use or even the threat of force was no longer legitimate, and that the strong must demonstrate restraint toward the weak. Gorbachev's idea of a New World included the major powers of the world, the United States, the Soviet Union, Europe, India, China, Japan, and Brazil.

He asked for cooperation on environmental protection, on debt relief for developing countries, on disarmament of nuclear weapons, on preservation of the Anti-Ballistic Missile Treaty, and on a convention for the elimination of chemical weapons. At the same time he promised the significant withdrawal of Soviet forces from Eastern Europe and Asia, as well as an end to the jamming of Radio Liberty.

In a speech in 1990, Gorbachev described a phenomenon that could be described as a global political awakening: "We are witnessing most profound social change. Whether in the East or the South, the West or the North, hundreds of millions of people, new nations and states, new public movements and ideologies have moved to the forefront of history. Broad-based and frequently turbulent popular movements have given expression, in a multidimensional and contradictory way, to a longing for independence, democracy and social justice. The idea of democratizing the entire world order has become a powerful socio-political force. At the same time, the scientific and technological revolution has turned many economic, food, energy, environmental, information and population problems, which only recently we treated as national or regional ones, into global problems. Thanks to the advances in mass media and means of transportation, the world seems to have become more visible and tangible. International communication has become easier than ever before."

What Gorbachev described was perceived as sound and just. To many, it seemed like a world without wars and prejudices. His words would describe the New World Order in its purest form, but as we know, things are not always what they seem to be.

In the press, Gorbachev was compared to Woodrow Wilson giving the Fourteen Points and to Franklin D. Roosevelt and Winston Churchill promoting the Atlantic Charter. His speech, while visionary, was to be approached with caution. He was seen as attempting a fundamental redefinition of international relationships, on economic and environmental levels. His support "for independence, democracy and social justice" was highlighted. But the principle message taken from his speech was that of a new world order based on pluralism, tolerance, and cooperation.

The Malta Conference on December 2–3, 1989 reinvigorated discussion of the new world order. New concepts arose such as the replacement of containment with superpower cooperation. This cooperation might then tackle problems such as reducing armaments and troop deployments, settling regional disputes, stimulating economic growth, lessening East-West trade restrictions, the inclusion of the Soviets in international economic institutions, and protecting the environment.

German reunification was seen as part of the new order. However, some saw it as more of a halt on the new era, and believed Malta to be a holding action on part of the superpowers designed to forestall the "new world order" because of the German question. Political change in Eastern Europe also arose on the agenda. The Eastern Europeans believed that the new world order didn't signify superpower leadership, but that superpower dominance was coming to an end.

In general, the new security structure arising from superpower cooperation seemed to indicate to observers that the new world order would be based on the principles of political liberty, self-determination, and non-intervention. This would mean an end to the sponsoring of military conflicts in third countries, restrictions on global arms sales, and greater engagement in the Middle East with particular concentration in Syria, Palestine, and Israel. The U.S. might use this opportunity to more emphatically promote human rights in China and South Africa.

Economically, debt relief was expected to be a significant issue, as competition would give way to cooperation. The U.S., Germany, and Japan would rise as the three agents of world growth. Meanwhile, the Soviet social and economic crisis was manifestly going to limit its ability to project power abroad, thus necessitating continued U.S. leadership.

Those assessing the results of the Conference, and how the pronouncements measured up to expectations, were underwhelmed. Bush was criticized for taking refuge behind the attitude of "status quo-plus" rather than presenting a full commitment to new world order. Others noted that Bush significantly failed to satisfy the out-of-control "soaring expectations" that Gorbachev's speeches of 1988 and 1990 unleashed.

"For a new type of progress throughout the world to become a reality, everyone must change. Tolerance is the alpha and omega of a new world order." Gorbachev, June 1990.

Gorbachev's initial formulation was wide ranging and idealistic, but his inability to overcome the internal crisis within his own nation, the Soviet Union, made it hard for him to live up to his own expectations.

Bush's vision was, in comparison, not less circumscribed: "A hundred generations have searched for this elusive path to peace, while a thousand wars raged across the span of human endeavor. Today that new world is struggling to be born, a world quite different from the one we've known." However, given the new unipolar status of the United States, Bush's vision was also realistic, stating: "there is no substitute for American leadership."

The Gulf War of 1991 was regarded as the first test of the new world order: "Now, we can see a new world coming into view. A world in which there is the very real prospect of a new world order." Bush stated. The Gulf war put this idea of collective cooperation to its first test.

Bush started to take the initiative from Gorbachev during the run-up to the Persian Gulf War, when he began to define the elements of the new world order in much the same way as Gorbachev did.

The Gulf War crisis refocused on superpower cooperation and regional crises. Economics, North-South problems, the integration of the Soviets into the international system, and the changes in economic and military polarity received greater attention.

The agreement by the Soviets to allow action against Saddam Hussein highlighted the new form of collective security. The Washington Post declared that this superpower cooperation demonstrates that the Soviet Union has joined the international community, and that in the new world order Saddam faced not just the U.S. but the international community itself. This new collective response to Saddam Hussein was nothing less than the new world order which Bush and other leaders were struggling to form. Even with this new Soviet agreement, definitive action against Saddam Hussein would not take place until 2003 and the second Bush presidency.

The 41st President, George H.W. Bush's September 11, 1990 speech, "Toward a New World Order" given to a joint session of Congress was seen as a pivotal moment for the movement. This time it was Bush, not Gorbachev, whose idealism was compared to Woodrow Wilson, and to Franklin D. Roosevelt at the creation of the UN. In his speech, Bush announced the following key points:

He promised a commitment of U.S. strength, leading the world toward an international rule of law, rather than the continual use of force. The Gulf crisis was a reminder that the U.S. must continue to lead, and that military strength does matter, but that the resulting new world order should make military force less important in the future.

He anticipated that a new Soviet -American partnership would emerge, making the world safe for democracy. However, skeptics countered that this partnership was unlikely, and that ideological tensions between the nations would remain, making them partners of convenience for specific and limited goals only. One caveat raised was that the new world order was based not on U.S.-Soviet cooperation, but really on Bush-Gorbachev cooperation, and that the personal diplomacy made the entire concept exceedingly fragile.

Future divisions were to be economic, not ideological, with the First and Second worlds cooperating to contain regional instability for Third world countries. Russia would become an ally against economic assaults from Asia, Islamic terrorism, and drugs from Latin America.

Restoration of German sovereignty and Cambodia's acceptance of the UN Security Council's peace plan on the day previous to the speech were seen as signs of what to expect in the new world order. While the reemergence of Germany and Japan as great powers, and the concurrent reform of the UN Security Council was seen as necessary for great power cooperation and reinvigoration of UN leadership

Europe was seen as taking the lead, while the U.S. was relegated to the sidelines. The rationale for U.S. presence on the continent was vanishing, and the Persian Gulf crisis was seen as incapable of rallying Europe. Instead Europe was had other plans. They were discussing a European Community, and relations with the USSR.

A small minority postulated a bi-polar new order of U.S. power and UN moral authority, the first being global policemen while the second would be considered a global judge and jury. The order would be collectivist, in which decisions and responsibility would be shared.

These were the common themes that emerged from Bush's speech, however, critics held that Bush was entirely too vague about what exactly his new order entailed.

Serious questions arose from the press including, "Would this mean a strengthened UN? Possibly new regional security arrangements in the gulf and elsewhere? Will the U.S. be willing to put its own military under international leadership?"

During the Gulf crisis, Mr. Bush rejected a UN command outright, however, when describing their goals, some Administration officials state that the U.S. must reduce its military burden and commitment. At other times, they appeared determined to seek new arrangements to preserve U.S. military supremacy and to justify new expenditures.

Needless to say, there was always contradiction and no one really knew exactly what leaders meant by the phrase "new world order.'

The American left was calling Bush's new world order a "rationalization for imperial ambitions" in the Middle East, while the right rejected the new security arrangements altogether and were in full denunciation about any possibility of UN revival.

Some predicted that the Gulf War would in fact be the demise of the new world order, as it pertains to the concept of UN peacekeeping, and the U.S.'s role as global policeman.

The deeper reality of the new world order was the United States' emergence as the single greatest power in a multi-polar world. Moscow was crippled by internal problems, unable to project any semblance of power abroad while the United States, although hampered by a declining economy, was superior militarily once again.

A common theme in most discussions is that the United States had acquired its dominant position in the international hierarchy due primarily to the decline of the Soviet Union. Bush himself has indicated that it is the new relationship with Moscow that created the possibility for his new order with it's essential features being not the values it is said to embody nor the principles upon which it is to be based, but that it has the United States at its center.

Washington's capacity to exert overwhelming military power and leadership over a multinational coalition sent chills down the backs of world leaders whenever America would "call for order."

The Iraq War of 2003 was viewed by the world and in the minds of most governments, as America's war. Then President George W. Bush (the 43rd President) chose to stake his political life on defeating Saddam Hussein.

An attack on Iraq would shatter Bush's alliance with the United Nations Security Council Members, prompting calls from some members saying that diplomacy should have been given more time, and that they will not allow a course of action that leaves America as the sole remaining superpower.

Bush forged on and once the casualties began to mount, he was called a warmonger, an imperialist and a bully. The new world order was overshadowed by the launch a Bush's controversial war.

Several academic assessments of the "new world order" were published following the Persian Gulf War, which was seen as the vessel in which great power cooperation and collective security would emerge as the new norms of the era.

John Lewis Gaddis, a Cold War historian, wrote in Foreign Affairs about what he saw as the key characteristics of the potential new order: unchallenged American primacy, increasing integration, resurgent nationalism and religiosity, a diffusion of security threats, and collective security. He casts the fundamental challenge as one of integration versus fragmentation, and the benefits and dangers associated with each.

Changes in communications, the international economic system, the nature of security threats, and the rapid spread of new ideas would prevent nations from retreating into isolation. In light of this, Gaddis saw a chance for the democratic peace predicted by liberal international theorists come closer to reality.

However, he illustrates that not only is the fragmentary pressure of nationalism manifest in the former Communist bloc countries and the Third World, but is also a considerable factor in the West.

Gaddis felt that the integration coming from the new order could aggravate ecological, demographic, and epidemic threats. National self-determination, leading to the breakup and reunification of states could signal abrupt shifts in the balance of power, with a destabilizing effect. Integrated markets, especially energy markets, would now be a security liability for the world economic system, as events affecting energy security in one part of the globe could threaten countries far removed from potential conflicts.

Finally, diffusion of these unintended security threats would require a new security paradigm, one involving low-intensity but more frequent deployment of peacekeeping troops, a mission that is hard to sustain under budgetary as well as public opinion pressure.

However, statesman Strobe Talbott wrote that it was only in the aftermath of the Persian Gulf War that the United Nations took a step toward redefining its role, one that would take into account both interstate relations and intrastate events. Furthermore, he asserted that it was only as an unintended postscript to Desert Storm that Bush gave meaning to the "new world order" slogan. But, by the end of the year Bush stopped talking about a new world order because he felt it suggested more enthusiasm for the changes sweeping the planet than he actually felt. He wanted, as an antidote to the uncertainties of the world, to stress the old verities of territorial integrity, national sovereignty and international stability.

The expectation of harmony of a new world order was widely shared by political and intellectual leaders. The Berlin wall had come down while communist regimes had collapsed. The United Nations would assume a new and significant importance while former Cold War rivals would engage in "new partnerships." Peacekeeping and peacemaking would therefore be the order of the day.

The euphoria emanating from the end of the Cold War generated an illusion of harmony for a time. The world became different in the early 1990's, but not necessarily more peaceful. Change was inevitable; progress was not. The illusion of harmony soon dissipated by the multiplication of ethnic conflicts and "ethnic cleansing," the breakdown of law and order, the emergence of new patterns of alliance and conflict among states and the intensification of religious fundamentalism. The world saw the end of diplomacy in Russia's relations with the West. The United Nations and the United States were unable to suppress bloody local conflicts, nor the increasing assertiveness of a rising China. In the five years after the Berlin wall came down, the word "genocide" was heard far too often.

Despite the criticisms of the new world order concept, ranging from its practical un-workability to its theoretical incoherence, Bill Clinton not only signed on to the idea of the "new world order," but dramatically expanded the concept beyond Bush's formulation. The essence of Clinton's election year critique was that Bush had done too little, not too much.

American intellectual Noam Chomsky, author of the 1994 book World Orders Old and New, describes the New World Order as a post-Cold-War era in which "the New World gives the orders".

Commenting on the 1999 US-NATO bombing of Serbia, he writes, "The aim of these assaults is to establish the role of the major imperialist powers--above all, the United States--as the unchallengeable arbiters of world affairs. The "New World Order" is precisely this: an international regime of unrelenting pressure and intimidation by the most powerful capitalist states against the weakest."

Viewed in retrospect, a 2001 paper in Presidential Studies Quarterly examined the idea of the "new world order" as it was presented by the Bush administration (mostly ignoring previous uses by Gorbachev). Their conclusion was that Bush really only ever had three firm aspects to the new world order:

1. Checking the offensive use of force.
2. Promoting collective security.
3. Great power cooperation.

These were not developed into a policy architecture, but came about incrementally as a function of domestic, personal, and global factors. Because of the somewhat overblown expectations for the new world order in the media, Bush was widely criticized for lacking vision.

The Gulf crisis is seen as the catalyst for Bush's development and implementation of the new world order concept. The authors note that before the crisis, the concept remained "ambiguous, nascent, and unproven" and that the United States had not assumed a leadership role with respect to the new order. Essentially, the Cold War's end was the permissive cause for the new world order, but the Persian Gulf crisis was the active cause.

Bush's motivation in heading into the Gulf War was based on the world making a clear choice, "either you were for aggression or you were against aggression".

The Gulf War was also framed as a test case for UN credibility. As a model for dealing with aggressors, it was believed that the United States ought to act in a way that others can trust, and thus get UN support. It was critical that the U.S. not look like it was throwing its weight around. Great power cooperation and UN support would collapse if the U.S. marched on unilaterally. However, practically, superpower cooperation was limited. For example, when the U.S. deployed troops to

Saudi Arabia, Soviet Foreign Minister Eduard Shevardnadze became furious at not being consulted.

By 1992, the U.S. was already abandoning the idea of collective action. The leaked draft of the 1992 Defense Guidance Report effectively confirmed this shift, as it called for a unilateral role for the U.S. in world affairs, focusing on preserving American dominance.

It was well-known that the U.S. had the strength and resources to pursue its own interests, but also had a responsibility to use its power in pursuit of the common good, as well as an obligation to lead and to be involved by creating predictability and stability in international relations. America need not be embroiled in every conflict, but ought to aid in developing multilateral responses to them by brokering disputes, in concert with equally committed partners.

Henry Kissinger stated in 1994, "The New World Order cannot happen without U.S. participation, as we are the most significant single component. Yes, there will be a New World Order, and it will force the United States to change its perceptions."

Iranian President Mahmoud Ahmadinejad has called for a new world order based on new ideas, saying the era of tyranny has come to a dead-end. In an exclusive interview with Islamic Republic of Iran Broadcasting (IRIB), Ahmadinejad noted that it is time to propose new ideologies for running the world. Iran's stated goal is to establish a new world order based on world peace, global collective security, reciprocity and justice.

Georgian President, Mikheil Saakashvili, has said "it's time to move from words to action because this is not going to go away. This nation is fighting for its survival, but we are also fighting for world peace and we are also fighting for a Future World Order."

Turkish President, Abdullah Gül, has said "I don't think you can control all the world from one center, there are big nations. There are huge populations. There is unbelievable economic development in some parts of the world. So what we have to do is, instead of unilateral actions, act all together, make common decisions and have consultations with the world. A new world order, if I can say it, should emerge."

The concept of a New World Order in its purest form was to be a good thing for everyone. It was originally designed to promote safety and prosperity for all. It was supposed to ensure that every person on the planet had an opportunity to succeed, raise their families in peace through freedom, while building a world based on mutual respect, love and togetherness for us all.

But in the end, corruption perverted it, as it always does, and the elite, super-wealthy, power hungry politicians and businessmen, like Barack Obama, Hillary Clinton and George Soros changed the beauty of a harmonic world into their own paradise, with the rest of us paying for their existence with our own.[4]

"Every aspect of
human technology has
a dark side, including
the bow and arrow."

Margaret Atwood

CHAPTER 4

THE DARK SIDE OF THE NWO

In 1782, the United States began using the magnificent seal, shown above, which is held by the office of the Secretary of State. The seal is used to signify the authenticity of state documents of the highest importance. The Great Seal, as it is referred to, is used as the national coat of arms of the U.S. It is also used on official documents such as U.S. passports, military insignia, embassy placards, and various flags. As a coat of arms, the design displays it's majestic colors, however, the Great Seal itself, once affixed to paper, is monochrome.

The reverse side of the Great Seal is emblazoned with an unfinished pyramid and a celestial looking eye within the triangle, called the Eye of Providence. The eye's primary function is to "watch and protect." The pyramid consists of 13 levels representing the 13 original states. The Latin phrase "novus ordo seclorum" has been on the reverse side of the Great Seal since its inception in 1782 and means "a new order of the ages." The other phrase, "Annuit cœptis" means the

Providence has "approved of (the) undertakings" for which the seal might have been used.

The base of the pyramid is inscribed with the Roman numeral date of MDCCLXXVI (1776) for the year of the U.S. Declaration of Independence. The reverse side of the Great Seal has never been cut for use as an actual seal, yet it appears on the back of the one-dollar bill.

I reference the Great Seal not only because of its beauty, but also because of the inscription on the back. For some, the phrase, "novus ordo seclorum" indicates that the New World Order (NWO) has possibly been around since the 1700's.

The previous chapter was a history of the New World Order and just like the United Nations and Globalism, it started with the purest of intentions. But as the old saying goes, "The road to hell is paved with good intentions." This is no different. The most powerful and wealthy believe that the existence of the planet is unsustainable. They have devised a plan which will ensure their existence, but the price of their success will be paid by the rest of us, the peasants of the world, if you will. This chapter will explain how an altruistic theory turned into something dark and sinister.

119

In the early years of the 1990's, the New World Order conspiracy belief was limited to two American countercultures. These were the anti-government, militant right and a sub-section of fundamentalist Christians, who were overly concerned with the end of times and the impending arrival of the Antichrist.

Skeptics began to observe that right-wing populist theories about a dark New World Order were being embraced by many. New information was seeping into the populace, bringing with it a newly defined period in the late 20th and early 21st centuries. The people of the United States, those who believed, began to actively prepare for an apocalyptic millennium as opposed to the peaceful, happy scenario they had come to expect.

Political scientists became alarmed, concerned about mass hysteria and the effects it could have on American politics. They were preparing for the worst scenarios ranging from widespread political alienation to escalating terrorism.

Progressives were in favor of the changing world views as it let them further their agenda of a world dominated by a Globalist and One World Government.

However, in the 21st century, the phrase NWO would bring to mind a dark and terrifying revelation of where our world is heading. Many believe that the NWO refers to the emergence of a totalitarian world government.

The phrase new world order was used repeatedly over the years in one form or another by world leaders but until recently, the phrase had no real meaning in the minds of the public. Today, however, the phrase sparks fear and is the source of many conspiracy theories.

The common theme emerging through America and the World was that the New World Order and the globalist agenda were conspiring to eventually rule the entire world with an authoritarian approach.

The NWO elites will force sovereign nations to adopt an all-inclusive propaganda whose ideology will recognize the elite establishment as the controllers of the New World and create a worldwide proletariat society for the rest of the world's population.

There are many influential, political, and just down-right filthy rich individuals who appear to be part of the inner circle of elites. They operate through various foundations and organizations with one purpose in mind. They intend to orchestrate chaos through significant political and financial crisis. They have been creating tragic world events, such as worldwide terrorism using the radical Islamic group known as ISIS and a lesser known group called Black Lives Matter (BLM), whose only purpose is to spread destruction and fear through intimidation throughout the world's population. This intentional fear they are ginning up within every person and nation will eventually give them the ability to achieve world domination by instituting Global Governance, which we will discuss in a later chapter.

The Red Scare which took place from 1947 to 1957, championed and lead by Senator Joseph McCarthy, was the promotion of fear invoked by a potential rise of communism or radical leftism. This paved the way for agitators of the American secular and Christian right, to spread unfounded fears of Freemasons, Illuminati, and Jews; convincing people that those groups were the driving force behind an "international communist conspiracy".

The perceived threat of an established atheistic state and collectivist world government, became known as the "Red Menace".

The Red Scare gave shape to the core ideas of the political right in the United States. They believed that the ideology of liberals and progressives, through a welfare-state agenda and international programs such as foreign aid, would lead to the gradual process of collectivism and would inevitably lead to nations being replaced with a communist one-world government.

This conclusion lead to the 1960's claim that the governments of both the United States and the Soviet Union were controlled by corporate internationalists, corrupt bankers, complicit politicians and the wealthy elites intent on using the U.N. as the vehicle to create an official and binding "One World Government".

Many intellectuals believed that the alleged New World Order agenda could be traced all the way back to the creation of the US Federal Reserve in 1913. The Reserve was led by international bankers, who later formed the Council on Foreign Relations in 1921, as an ostensibly shadow government. At the time, "international bankers" would've been interpreted by many as a reference to the "international Jewish banking conspiracy" masterminded by the Rothschild family.

The Rothschilds descended from Mayer Amschel Rothschild, a court Jew to the German Landgraves of Hesse-Kassel, in the Free City of Frankfurtan. Mayer Amschel Rothschild was born February 23, 1744 and died on September 19, 1812. He was a German Jewish banker and the founder of the Rothschild banking dynasty. Referred to as the "founding father of international finance," Rothschild was ranked seventh on the 2005 Forbes magazine list of "The Twenty Most Influential Businessmen of All Time".

During the 19th century, the Rothschild family held the largest private fortune in the world. Today, they are still believed to be the wealthiest family in human history, and very influential in matters of the world. Many believe that they are the main creators of the modern day NWO.

The term "New World Order" is used most often by highly secretive elites committed to the termination of all national sovereignties. After the fall of communism in the early 1990's, the American far right seamlessly switched its angst from communism to globalism and the New World

Order. This shift was, in part, due to a growing right-wing populist opposition to corporate internationalism, and became the basis for the underlying idea of an apocalyptic millenarian paradigm.

The 41st President of the United States, George H. W. Bush, delivered a speech during a joint session of the U.S. Congress on September 11, 1990. In the speech Bush described his objectives for a post-Cold War global governance in cooperation with post-Soviet states. He stated:

"Until now, the world we've known has been a world divided--a world of barbed wire and concrete block, conflict and cold war. Now, we can see a new world coming into view. A world in which there is the very real prospect of a new world order. In the words of Winston Churchill, a world order in which 'the principles of justice and fair play ... protect the weak against the strong ...' A world where the United Nations, freed from cold war stalemate, is poised to fulfill the historic vision of its founders. A world in which freedom and respect for human rights find a home among all nations."

Progressives denounced the new world order suggested by President Bush as a rationalization of American imperialism around the world.

Conservatives rejected any new security arrangements altogether and fulminated about the possibility of UN involvement within the U.S.

Christians and the secular hard right received President Bush's announcement of his new foreign policy with disdain. Bush's intention to help build a New World Order surged through them like a nuclear explosion. They believed that Bush's statement represented the dreaded collectivist One World Government.

Christians saw this as a Bush betrayal, signaling the End of Times propagated by a major world leader. Secular anti-communists saw this as a bold attempt to destroy US sovereignty and impose a tyrannical collectivist system run by the United Nations.

American televangelist Pat Robertson, with his 1991 best-selling book "The New World Order", became the most prominent Christian communicator of the theories involved in the creation of the NWO.

He describes a scenario in which Wall Street, the Federal Reserve System, the Council on

Foreign Relations, the Bilderberg Group and the Trilateral Commission would manipulate and control events behind the scenes while gingerly nudging people in the direction of a one world government.

The galvanizing of right-wing populist groups led to the rise of a militia movement, which spread its anti-government ideology during speeches at rallies and meetings, through books and videos, satellite radio, and computer bulletin boards.

Radio shows and the Internet delivered viral propaganda which effectively promoted their extremist political ideas about the New World Order. From the mid 1990's on, information on the NWO spread like a "virus" to a new, large audience willing to listen for the first time.

Hollywood television shows and films also played a large role in introducing the NWO conspiracy-thrillers to audiences. People began to believe the stories about Black helicopters, their government's possible betrayal, FEMA "concentration camps" and more. For decades these ideas were confined to radical right-wing subcultures but soon became known to all.

The 21st century, and specifically during the late-2000 financial crisis, many politicians and pundits would use the term "new world order" to advance their idea of comprehensive reform of the global financial system.

These declarations instead had the unintended consequence of providing fresh fodder for NWO opponents, which culminated in talk show host Sean Hannity stating on his Fox News Channel program "Hannity" that the "conspiracy theorists were right". Hannity, Fox News, and the former opinion show of Glenn Beck, were repeatedly criticized by progressive media watchdog groups, for not "giving life" to the New World Order conspiracy theories of the radical right, but possibly agitating the public at large.

In 2009, American film directors Luke Meyer and Andrew Neel released a critically acclaimed documentary called "New World Order", which explores the conspiracy theorists. One in particular is an American radio host Alex Jones. Jones has been committed to exposing and opposing what he perceived to be an emerging New World Order.

There are many systemic conspiracy theories through which the concept of a New

World Order is viewed. I will detail a few of them here.

Since the 19th century, many Christian theologists predicted a globalist conspiracy which would impose a despotic New World Order governing body as described by prophecies in the Bible referencing the "end of times." They claim that making a deal with the Devil to gain wealth and power creates pawns in a supernatural game of chess, moving humanity into accepting a reformist world government. This new government would be built on the spiritual foundation of a world religion, eventually creating the cult of an "Unholy Trinity" of Satan, the Antichrist and the False Prophet.

In many contemporary Christian conspiracy theories, the False Prophet will be either the last pope of the Catholic Church, a guru from the New Age movement, or even the leader of an elite fundamentalist Christian organization, while the Antichrist will be either the President of the U.S. or possibly the European Union, the Secretary General of the U.N., or even the Caliph of a pro-Islamic state.

Freemasonry is one of the world's oldest secular fraternal organizations. They originated from the stone-mason's guilds of the 15th century and over the years many allegations have been directed towards them. It was believed that the Freemasons have been conspiring to bring about a New World Order, a world government organized according to Masonic principles and governed by the Freemasons.

Freemasonry describes itself as a "'beautiful system of morality, veiled in allegory and illustrated by symbols". The Masonic symbol, shown above, is drawn using the tools of stone-masons: the square and compasses, the level and plumb rule, among others. While not all Masonic lodges have the same symbol, however, attached to each symbol was a moral lesson.

The cabalistic nature of the Masonic symbolism and rituals were what led to Freemasons being accused of secretly practicing Satanism in the late 18th century. It became a concern that the intentions of the Freemasonry were to alter religions and governments in order to take over the world.

In the 1890's, French author Léo Taxil wrote a series of books excoriating the Freemasonry, suggesting that lodges were worshiping Lucifer as the Supreme Being. Taxil later admitted that his claims were all a hoax, however, they were still believed and repeated by numerous conspiracy theorists, having a huge influence on the anti-Masonic claims about Freemasonry.

Other conspiracies involved the Founding Fathers of the United States, such as George Washington and Benjamin Franklin. It was claimed that they were interweaving sacred Masonic geometric designs into American society. The claim was that these designs could be found on the Great Seal of the U.S., the dollar bill, and the architecture of National Mall landmarks instituting a master plan to create the first "Masonic government" in the U.S. as a model for the coming New World Order.

Freemasons dispute claims of a Masonic conspiracy. The Freemasonry claims to be promoting a philosophical theory and places no power in occult symbols. They claim that the drawing of symbols is not a means of garnering power.

The accusation that Freemasonry has a hidden agenda to establish a Masonic government has never been conclusively proven, however many believe the accusations.

On May 1, 1776, a university professor in Upper Bavaria, Germany named Adam Weishaupt founded The Order of the Illuminati, a secret society of the Enlightenment era.

We have all grown up hearing the term Illuminati, but most believed that they were only a conspiracy and never existed in the first place. However, we were wrong.

The Illuminati Order consisted of advocates for free-thought, liberalism, secularism, republicanism, and gender equality. They recruited members from German Masonic Lodges, who sought to teach rationalism at secret schools.

In 1785, they were infiltrated and suppressed by the government agents of Charles Theodore, Elector of Bavaria. His purpose was to neutralize the threat of secret societies from ever becoming breeding grounds for conspiracies that could overthrow the Bavarian monarchy and its Roman Catholic religion.

In the late 18th century, conservative conspiracy theorists speculated that the Illuminati had actually survived Bavaria's suppression and were considered the masterminds of the French Revolution and the Reign of Terror. The Illuminati were accused of being radical, attempting to secretly choreograph a revolutionary tsunami not just in Europe but the rest of the world as well. Their perceived plan was to spread anti-clericalism, anti-monarchism, and anti-patriarchalism, as well as other radical ideas of the Enlightenment to create a world "based on the priority of human mind" and cult of reason.

During the 19th century, the Illuminati became a real concern and fear for the European ruling classes, and their oppressive reactions to their fear would provoke the very revolutions they sought to prevent.

During the inter-war period of the 20th century, propagandists not only popularized the myth of an Illuminati conspiracy but claimed that it was a secret society serving Jewish elites who were supposedly propping up both finance capitalism and Soviet communism with the intention to divide and rule the world.

In the early 1900's, American evangelists and other conspiracy theorists within the fundamentalist Christian movement in the U.S. emerged as a backlash against the principles of secular humanism, modernism, and liberalism. They became the main disseminators of Illuminati conspiracy theories. Right-wing populists, began speculating that some collegiate fraternities, gentleman's clubs, and think tanks such as the Council on Foreign Relations and the Trilateral Commission, and the American upper class were sponsors of the Illuminati, which they accuse of plotting to create a New World Order through a one-world government.

Whereas, there is no evidence that the Bavarian Illuminati survived its suppression in 1785, their name is still being used today. Several present-day fraternal groups openly use the name "Illuminati" claiming to be descendants of the original Bavarian Order. Some of these groups use a variation on the name "The Illuminati Order" while others, such as the Ordo Templi Orientis, have "Illuminati" as a level within the hierarchy of their organization.

However, these present-day groups have garnered no significant political power or influence, but simply use the dubious link to the Bavarian Illuminati as a means of attracting membership.

The Protocols of the Elders of Zion is an anti-Semitic fabrication, published in Russian in 1903. It alleged a Judeo-Masonic conspiracy to achieve world dominance. The text claims to be a written record of secret meetings of Jewish masterminds, who embraced Freemasonry, to rule the world on behalf of all Jews because they believe themselves to be the chosen people of God.

The Protocols reflect themes similar to the criticisms of Enlightenment liberalism by conservative aristocrats who support monarchies and state religions. The interpretation intended by the printing of The Protocols is that "if one strips away the layers of the Masonic conspiracy, past the Illuminati, one will find a rotten Jewish core."

The Protocols were responsible for the fueling of numerous anti-Semitic and anti-Masonic mass hysterias of the 20th century. They were also influential in the development of a few NWO conspiracies and appear repeatedly in certain contemporary conspiracy literature.

However, "The Times" of London exposed the protocols as a forgery, fabricated for the secret police of the Russian Empire to be used as counter-revolutionary propaganda prior to the 1905 Russian Revolution.

In 1917, President Woodrow Wilson asked a group of New York academics to provide options for the foreign policy of the United States during the inter-war period. Originally the group consisted of a handful of American and British scholars and diplomats, but in June of 1918, a subsequent group was formed which included 108 New York financiers, manufacturers and international lawyers. The group was organized by Nobel Peace Prize recipient and U.S. Secretary of State, Elihu Root, and officially became the Council on Foreign Relations on July 29, 1921.

The first of the council's projects was a quarterly journal launched in September of 1922, called Foreign Affairs. In July 1973, The Trilateral Commission was founded through the initiative of American banker and businessman, David Rockefeller, the chairman of the Council on Foreign Relations at the time.

The Council is a private organization established to advance closer cooperation among the United States, Europe and Japan. The Trilateral Commission is widely viewed as a extension to the Council on Foreign Relations.

In the 1960's, right-wing populist groups like the John Birch Society, were the first to spread an ultraconservative business nationalist critique of corporate advocates networked through organizations such as the Council on Foreign Relations and were financed by "elite international bankers" that supposedly have been plotting from the late 19th century to impose an oligarchic new world order through the global financial system.

Anti-global conspiracy theorist began to fear that international bankers were planning to eventually destroy the freedom of the U.S. by handing our national sovereignty over to a strengthened Bank for International Settlements.

Larry McDonald, a U.S. Congressman who represented District 7 in Georgia from 1975 until the day he was killed while on Korean Air Lines flight 007 which was shot down by Soviet interceptors. McDonald, a loyal Democrat, succeeded Robert Welch as Chairman of The John Birch Society. He wrote the foreword for Gary

Allen's 1976 book "The Rockefeller File", wherein he stated:

"The drive of the Rockefellers and their allies is to create a one-world government, combining super-capitalism and Communism under the same tent, all under their control ... Do I mean conspiracy? Yes I do. I am convinced there is such a plot, international in scope, generations old in planning, and incredibly evil in intent."

David Rockefeller wrote this in his 2002 autobiography: "For more than a century ideological extremists at either end of the political spectrum have seized upon well-publicized incidents ... to attack the Rockefeller family for the inordinate influence they claim we wield over American political and economic institutions. Some even believe we are part of a secret cabal working against the best interests of the United States, characterizing my family and me as 'internationalists' and of conspiring with others around the world to build a more integrated global political and economic structure--one world, if you will. If that's the charge, I stand guilty, and I am proud of it."

Michael Barkun, retired professor of political science at the Maxwell School of

Citizenship and Public Affairs, Syracuse University, specialized in political extremism. Barkun argues that David Rockefeller's statement was partly facetious and partly serious. The desire, at the time, was to encourage trilateral cooperation among the U.S., Europe, and Japan, for example. This idea was to be a hallmark of the internationalist wing of the Republican Party, known as "Rockefeller Republicans" in honor of Nelson Rockefeller.

The statement, however, was taken at face value and was widely cited by conspiracy theorists as proof that the Council on Foreign Relations did indeed use its influence on American presidents, senators, and representatives to manipulate them into supporting a New World Order in the form of a one-world government.

In 1928, H. G. Wells wrote the book "The Open Conspiracy" and in 1940, wrote "The New World Order."

"The Open Conspiracy" promoted cosmopolitanism and offered blueprints for a world revolution and world brain to establish a technocratic world state and planned economy.

Wells would later warn in his book "The New World Order" that: "... when the struggle seems to be drifting definitely towards a world social democracy, there may still be very great delays and disappointments before it becomes an efficient and beneficent world system. Countless people ... will hate the new world order, be rendered unhappy by the frustration of their passions and ambitions through its advent and will die protesting against it. When we attempt to evaluate its promise, we have to bear in mind the distress of a generation or so of malcontents, many of them quite gallant and graceful-looking people."

Wells' books were successful in providing a second meaning to the term "new world order", one used by state socialist supporters and anti-communist opponents for generations to come.

However, despite the popularity of his ideas, Wells would fail to exert a deep and lasting influence due to his inability to concentrate his energies on a more direct appeal to elite groups who would, ultimately, have to coordinate in order to install the Wellsian new world order.

Inexplicably, the New World Order conspiracy is increasingly being embraced and used as propaganda by New Age occultists, who are generally people bored by rationalism and drawn to stigmatized knowledge, such as astrology, alternative medicine, spiritualism, mysticism, and theosophy.

New Age conspiracy theorists claim that globalists who plot on behalf of the New World Order are simply misusing occultism for unscrupulous means, such as adopting December 21, 2012 as the exact date for the establishment of the New World Order with the sole intention of taking advantage of the supposed 2012 cataclysmic events which would transform humanity. As we all know, this event never took place.

Skeptics argue that the connection between conspiracy theorists and occultists grew from their common deceptive premises. First, any widely accepted belief must be false, while stigmatized knowledge must be true. The result was a self-referential network in which, for example, some UFO religionists might actually promote anti-Jewish phobias while some anti-Semites might practice the Peruvian religious belief of shamanism.

The Brave New World is an interesting theory and consists of people who hold anti-scientific views, reject scientific methodology and do not accept that science generates universal knowledge. Neo-Luddite's are considered to be anti-technology, or those who dislike or have a difficult time understanding and using modern science and technology. However, both emphasize technology forecasting, a measure to predict the future characteristics of useful technological machines, procedures or techniques, in their New World Order conspiracy theories.

They believe that global elites are mostly reactionary modernists who pursue a trans-humanist agenda by using human enhancement technologies to become a "post-human ruling caste." This would propel them on a rapid course to technological singularity.

Consider for a moment what this might mean. A technological singularity is a hypothetical event in which, let's use in this case, an upgradeable computer running software-based artificial general intelligence (AGI) that could successfully perform any intellectual task that a human being could perform. This computer then enters into a 'runaway reaction' of self-improvement cycles, resulting in a new and more intelligent generation appearing more rapidly with each cycle. This causes an intelligence explosion which result in a powerful super-intelligence that would, qualitatively, far surpass all human intelligence. This would signal the end of the human era, as the new super-intelligence would continue to upgrade itself and would advance technologically at an incomprehensible rate. In theory, you would then have a point of separation where events accelerate at such a rapid pace that normal un-enhanced humans will not be able to understand the rapid changes occurring in the world around them.

Conspiracy theorists fear the outcome of a technological singularity will be either the emergence of a Brave New World-like dystopia or the extinction of the human species.

Democratic trans-humanists counter that many influential members of the United States establishment are actually bio-conservatives who are staunchly opposed to human enhancement, as demonstrated by the 43rd President, George W. Bush's Council on Bioethics which proposed an international treaty prohibiting human cloning and germ-line engineering.

Just as there are overlapping or conflicting theories among conspiracists about the nature of the New World Order, so are there several beliefs about how its architects and planners will implement it:

Conspiracists speculate that the New World Order is being implemented gradually, citing the creation of the following organizations listed in chronological order.

The U.S. Federal Reserve in 1913

The League of Nations in 1919

The International Monetary Fund 1944

The United Nations in 1945

The World Bank in 1945

The World Health Organization in 1948

The European Union in 1993

The World Trade Organization in 1998

The African Union in 2002 and

The Union of South American Nations in 2008 as proof of a gradual implementation.

An increasingly popular conspiracy theory among American right-wing populists is that the North American Union and the Amero currency, the counterpart to the Euro, proposed by the Council on Foreign Relations and its counterparts in Mexico and Canada, will be the next steps in the implementation of the New World Order.

The theory holds that a group of mysterious and mostly nameless international elites are indeed planning to replace the U.S. federal government with a transnational government. Therefore, conspiracy theorists believe the borders between Mexico, Canada and the United States are in the process of being erased, covertly, by a group of globalists whose ultimate goal is to replace national governments in Washington, D.C., Ottawa and Mexico City with a European-style political union.

Skeptics argue that the North American Union exists only on academic and/or policy papers published each year and advocate all manner of idealistic but ultimately unrealistic approaches to social, economic and political problems. They claim that most of these are passed but are eventually filed away and forgotten by junior staffers in congressional offices. I think considering what is happening right now, it is safe to say that there is more here than meets the eye.

For example, in March 2009, as a result of the financial crisis of 2007 and 2008, the People's Republic of China and the Russian Federation urgently pressed for consideration of a new international reserve currency and the United Nations Conference on Trade and Development proposed greatly expanding the I.M.F.'s special drawing rights. Conspiracy theorists fear these proposals were a call for the U.S. to adopt a global currency for a New World Order.

In light of the fact that national governments and global institutions have been mostly ineffective in managing worldwide problems that go beyond the capacity of individual nations to solve, some political scientists argue that regionalism will be the major force in the coming decades, with power centers around Brussels, Belgium in western Europe; Washington D.C. in the western hemisphere; Beijing, China in east Asia; and finally, Moscow, Russia in eastern Europe.

As such, the E.U., the Shanghai Cooperation Organization, and the G-20 will likely become more influential as time progresses. The question then is not whether global governance is gradually emerging, but rather how will these regional powers interact with one another.

Those who are strong believers in a right to keep and bear arms, are extremely fearful that the passing of any gun control legislation will be the catalyst which will lead to the abolishment of personal gun ownership and eventually gun confiscation. They also believe that the refugee camps of emergency management agencies such as

FEMA will be used for the internment of anyone who doesn't adhere to their imposed confiscation.

Those concerned with surveillance abuse believe that the New World Order is being implemented by the cult of intelligence at the core of the surveillance industrial complex through mass surveillance and the use of Social Security numbers, the bar-coding of retail goods with Universal Product Code markings, and, most recently, Radio-frequency identification (RFID) tagging by microchip implants.

Those concerned with Big Brother watching, claim that corporations and the government are planning to track every move of consumers and citizens with RFID as the latest step toward a 1984-like surveillance state.

Christian conspiracy theorists believe that spy chips must be resisted because with modern database and communications technologies, coupled with point of sale data-capture equipment and sophisticated ID and authentication systems, now make it possible to require a biometrically associated number or mark to make purchases. They consider this to be too closely related to The Mark Of The Beast, as mentioned in the Bible.

Civil libertarians argue that the privatization of surveillance and the rise of the surveillance-industrial complex in the United States does raise legitimate concerns about the erosion of privacy. However, skeptics of mass surveillance caution that such concerns should be disentangled from secular paranoia about Big Brother or religious hysteria about the Antichrist.

In January 2002, the Defense Advanced Research Projects Agency (DARPA) established the Information Awareness Office (IAO) whose goal was to bring together several DARPA projects focused on applying information technology to counter threats to national security. Following public criticism that the development of these technologies could potentially lead to a mass surveillance system, the IAO was de-funded by the United States Congress in 2003. The second source of controversy involved IAO's logo, which depicted the "all-seeing" Eye of Providence atop of a pyramid looking down over the globe, accompanied by the Latin phrase "scientia est potentia" meaning "knowledge is power." Although DARPA removed the logo from its website, it left a lasting impression on privacy advocates. It also inflamed theories, that the "eye and pyramid" were the Masonic symbol of the Illuminati.

Conspiracy theorists believe that the New World Order will also be implemented through the use of human population control in order to more easily monitor and control the movement of individuals. The means range from stopping the growth of human societies through reproductive health and family planning programs, which promote abstinence, contraception and abortion, or intentionally reducing the bulk of the world population through genocides by mongering unnecessary wars, or engineered plagues, emergent viruses and the tainting of vaccines, and through environmental disasters by controlling the weather using the High Frequency Active Auroral Research Program (HAARP), chem-trails, etc.

Conspiracy theorists argue that globalists plotting on behalf of a New World Order are neo-Malthusians, who advocate population control programs, to ensure resources for current and future populations. By using overpopulation and climate change fears, founded or not, they create public support for coercive population control and ultimately world government.

Skeptics argue that fears of population control can be traced back to the traumatic legacy of the eugenics movement's "war against the weak" in the United States during the first decades of the 20th century but also the Second Red Scare in the U.S. during the late 1900's and 1900's, and to a lesser extent in the 1960's, when activists on the far right of American politics routinely opposed public health programs, notably water fluoridation, mass vaccination and mental health services, by asserting they were all part of a far-reaching plot to impose a socialist or communist regime. Their views were influenced by opposition to a number of major social and political changes that had happened in recent years: the growth of internationalism, particularly the United Nations and its programs; the introduction of social welfare provisions, particularly the various programs established by the New Deal; and government efforts to reduce inequalities in the social structure of the U.S..

William Domhoff, the author of a book entitled "Who Rules America", seems to believe that the United States is ruled from behind the scenes by a conspiratorial elite with secret desires, like changing the government system or put the country under the control of a world government. Domhoff notes that most conspiracy theorists changed their focus to the United Nations as the likely controlling force in a New World Order, but as the U.N. seems to be powerless, coupled with the moderates being unwilling to give it any legitimacy, it's role does have limitations.

Although skeptical of a New World Order conspiracy, political scientist David Rothkopf argues in the 2008 book "Superclass: The Global Power Elite and the World They Are Making," that the world population of 6 billion people is currently being governed by an elite class of about 6,000 individuals.

Until the late 20th century, the powerful world governments provided most of the superclass, accompanied by a few others, such as, the Pope of the Catholic Church, the Rothschild, the Rockefellers and various other wealthy Industrialists. According to Rothkopf, in the early 21st century, economic influence, fueled by the volatile expansion of international trade, travel and communication, rules. Leaders in international business, finance and the defense industry not only influence the superclass, they are generally given elite positions within their governments. They move freely between these high-power positions then back to private life largely unnoticed by elected officials, including the U.S. Congress, who remain blissfully ignorant when it comes to the affairs beyond their own borders. He insists that the disproportional influence of the superclass over national policy, albeit productive, is also extremely self-serving. Very few of the superclass or elites ever object to the corruption and oppressive governments and their actions, provided they can do business in these countries.

Some conspiracy theorists go further even than Rothkopf. They view the world as warfare between secret societies and other scholars who have studied the global power elite, by claiming that established upper-class families with "old money" who founded and financed the Bilderberg Group, Council on Foreign Relations, The Trilateral Commission, and similar think tanks and private clubs, as conspirators plotting to impose a totalitarian New World Order through the implementation of an authoritarian world government. The NWO would be controlled by the United Nations and a global central bank. This would maintain the political power of the elites through efforts such as the financialization of the economy, regulation and restrictions on free speech by the elites who own most of the media, mass surveillance, widespread use of state terrorism, and an all-encompassing propaganda movement that would create a cult of personality around a puppet world leader.

Marxists, being skeptical of right-wing populist conspiracies, accuse the global power elites of looking out only for themselves and not considering what is in the best interests of the rest of the world. Marxists argue that the superclass are plutocrats, only interested in imposing a neoliberal or neoconservative new world order through the implementation of global capitalism utilizing economic and military coercion to protect the interests of multi-nationalist corporations and the elites.

Skeptics of the NWO conspiracists accuse them of indulging in a misconception, believing that significant facts of history are sinister; conspiracism, a world view that centrally places conspiracy theories in the unfolding of history, rather than social and economic forces; and paranoia through the acceptance of fears from any source whatsoever.

William Domhoff, being a research professor in psychology and sociology who studies theories of power, writes the following in a March 2005 essay entitled "There Are No Conspiracies":

"There are several problems with a conspiratorial view that doesn't fit with what we know about power structures. First, it assumes that a small handful of wealthy and highly educated people somehow develop an extreme psychological desire for power that leads them to do things that don't fit with the roles they seem to have. For example, that rich capitalists are no longer out to make a profit, but to create a one-world government. Or that elected officials are trying to get the Constitution suspended so they can assume dictatorial powers. These kinds of claims go back many decades now, and it is always said that it is really going to happen this time, but it never does. Since these claims have proved wrong dozens of times by now, it makes more sense to assume that leaders act for their usual reasons, such as profit-seeking motives and institutionalized roles as elected officials. Of course they want to make as much money as they can, and be elected by huge margins every time, and that can lead them to do many unsavory things, but nothing in the ballpark of creating a one-world government or suspending the Constitution."

Over the last two decades, a far-right conspiracy of self-proclaimed "Patriots" has emerged in which the United States government itself is viewed as a mortal threat to everything from the Constitution to the survival of the human race. This conspiracy which has been accompanied by the continuous growth of Patriot groups, kicked into overdrive with the 2008 election of President Barack Obama. Right or wrong, Obama is seen by Patriots as a foreign-born Manchurian candidate sent by forces of the so-called "New World Order" to destroy American sovereignty and institute one-world socialist government.

Concerned that conspiracy theories about a New World Order might motivate the engagement of a leaderless resistance, such as domestic terrorist incidents like the Oklahoma City bombing and the ever-growing mass murders taking place around the world, Michael Barkun writes:

"The danger lies less in such beliefs themselves ... than in the behavior they might stimulate or justify. As long as the New World Order appeared to be almost but not quite a reality, devotees of conspiracy theories could be expected to confine their activities to propagandizing. On the other hand, should they believe that the prophesied evil day had in fact arrived, their behavior would become far more difficult to predict."

Richard T. Hughes, a professor of religion and the renowned author of "Christian America and the Kingdom of God", warns that "No religious idea has greater potential for shaping global politics in profoundly negative ways than the new world order". In a February 2011 article entitled "Revelation, Revolutions, and the Tyrannical New World Order" Hughes writes the following:

"The crucial piece of this puzzle is the identity of the Antichrist, the tyrannical figure who both leads and inspires the new world order. For many years, rapture theologians identified the Soviet Union as the Antichrist. But after Sept. 11, they became quite certain that the Antichrist was closely connected with the Arab world and the Muslim religion. This means, quite simply, that for rapture theologians, Islam stands at the heart of the tyrannical "new world order." Precisely here we discover why the idea of a "new world order" has such potential to move global politics in profoundly negative directions, for rapture theologians typically welcome war with the Islamic world." As Bill Moyers wrote of the rapture theologians, "A war with Islam in the Middle East is not something to be feared but welcomed, an essential conflagration on the road to redemption."

Further, rapture theologians co-opt the United States as a tool in their cosmic vision, a tool God will use to smite the Antichrist and the enemies of righteousness. This is why Tim LaHaye, co-author of a best-selling series of end-times books, could lend such strong support to the American invasion and occupation of Iraq. By virtue of that war, LaHaye believed, Iraq would become "a focal point of end-times events." Even more disturbing is the fact that rapture theologians blissfully would open the door to a nuclear holocaust, as they have always held that "God will destroy his enemies at the end of time in the Great Battle of Armageddon". As one prophecy writer put it, "The holocaust of atomic war would fulfill the prophecies."

Taking into account the events taking place in 2016 in America and around the world, I would have to say that I am not sure which I like least, the idea of Islam being the anti-Christ or the New World Order which the elites are planning for the world. Both are terrifying prospect to me and should be to you, as well.[5]

"Civilization must stand up and combat the current collapse of governance, the rise of violence, and the spread of chaos and fear in many parts of the world."

Rudy Giuliani

CHAPTER 5

GLOBAL GOVERNANCE

A Global Governance will consist of a group of political transnational's who will manage the coordinated responses and strategies throughout the world in an effort to resolve conflicts and problems that arise between one or more areas or regions.

Global governance will involve multiple agencies or institutions in an effort at maintaining worldwide control. These institutions or agencies might include but are not limited to the United Nations, the International Criminal Court, the World Bank, the World Health Organization, the World Trade Organization, etc., in an effort to achieve a consolidated power with which to enforce compliance.

The existence of a global governance can only be maintained through the globalization of all regimes of power: politically, economically and culturally.

The term "global governance" refers to the process of designating laws, rules, or regulations intended for use on a global scale.

The system of a global political relationship is not necessarily fully integrated, yet the partnership between the regimes of global governance is not without significance. The system's common dominant organizational form is derived from a bureaucratic rationale of standardized acceptance, coordination and forced compliance. It is common to all modern regimes of political power and frames the transition from traditional national sovereignty to one of global sovereignty.

Simply put, the definition of world governance is an ideology that will remove the rights of individual nations and assign them to the global society of the New World Order under the control of the United Nations.

Traditionally, the governments of individual nations have been concentrating simply on governing through political authority, institutions, and, ultimately, control. Traditional governance implies that sovereign nations can coordinate and control those within their borders through the ability to enforce, by force if necessary, their decisions and desired outcomes. However, some have argued that "global governance" is required to regulate the interdependent relations through an overarching political authority such as an international system, leading to the development of a "global public policy".

Adil Najam, a scholar on the subject at the Pardee School of Global Studies at Boston University has defined global governance simply as "the management of global processes in the absence of global government." According to Thomas G. Weiss, director of the Ralph Bunche Institute for International Studies and editor from 2000 to 2005 for the journal "Global Governance: A Review of Multilateralism and International Organizations" states that, "Global governance, can be good, bad, or indifferent and refers to concrete cooperative problem-solving arrangements, many of which increasingly involve not only the United Nations but also international secretariats and other non-state actors". In other words, global governance refers to the way in which global affairs are managed.

A single organization may be given the leading role on a given issue; for example, the World Trade Organization (WTO) would ultimately shape world trade affairs, while the World Health Organization (WHO) would dictate policy on health related concerns. Therefore, global governance is thought to be an international process of consensus which would generate guidelines and agreements that affect national governments and international corporations.

In short, global governance may be defined as; the structuring of formal and informal institutions, mechanisms, relationships, and processes between once sovereign nations, markets, citizens and organizations in which collective interests on a global scale are articulated. Duties, obligations and privileges are established, and differences are mediated through global elites.

The dissolution of the Soviet Union in 1991 marked the end of a long period in history which was based primarily on the "balance of powers" being the accepted norm. The model of national security, for example, while still in place for most governments, is gradually giving way to an emerging collective conscience.

The post-Cold War world of the 1990's saw a new paradigm emerge based on a number of issues:

1. The growing idea of globalization became a significant theme and with the subsequent weakening of nations, a gradual acceptance of global regulatory control was deemed necessary since national or regional levels of cooperation were no longer working effectively.

2. The introduction of concerns for the environment, relating to the climate and biodiversity, received universal acceptance at the Earth Summit and symbolized a new approach that was soon to be expressed conceptually by the term "Global Commons", which refers to pooled, international natural resources.

3. The emergence of conflicts over standards relating to trade and the environment, property rights, and public health, created conflicts which continued the debate and raised the question of arbitration among equally legitimate departments of the governance system. Although often limited in scope, these conflicts are nevertheless symbolically powerful as they raise the question of the principles and institutions of arbitration.

4. Developing countries, after having entered the global economy, increasingly questioned the international standards of the First World Nations. They found it hard to accept that the industrialized countries continued to hold onto power and give priority to their own interests. Challenges also came from civilized societies which considers the international governance system to be the real seat of power. These societies maintained their rejection of both the principles and procedures of global governance.

There are those who believe that the world structure depends heavily on the establishment of global governance. However, the idea is becoming far more complicated. The original formulation was about regulating and limiting the individual power of states, in order to avoid disturbing the status quo. However, the intent of today's world governance is to have a collective influence on the world's destiny by establishing a regulatory system with varying interactions that exceeds the sphere of state action. Liberal democracy and the political blending of the entire planet should make it easier to establish a one world governance system that goes beyond market indifference and democratic peace.

For those who support the establishment of global governance, their belief is based on the difficulty of achieving equitable development on a world scale. They believe that in order to secure peace and harmony for all human beings, in all parts of the world, the conditions allowing a decent and meaningful life requires enormous human energies and far-reaching changes in policies. The task is ever more demanding as our world faces intensifying difficulties, each calling for urgent attention.

Lack of tolerance for inequalities and the growing demand for redistribution creates a contradiction between property rights and human rights. In many cases, globalization serves to accentuate the discrepancies rather than being a force to bring the parties together. Responsibility must extend to regional and International governments when balancing the needs of its citizenry.

As growing awareness of the impact of globalization becomes more prevalent and opposition begins to take hold, a rapidly growing number of movements and organizations have taken the debate to an international level. As more nations and citizens come to realize the dark intentions of globalism, they have begun to reject it in huge numbers, with the exception of the elites and their ilk.

For global governance and globalism to become sustainable, it is important that populations see the benefits instead of the implications. Governing bodies must get together to agree on their goals so that the process of governing is seen as legitimate. So far, this isn't happening. There are just too many egos involved, creating a "crisis of purpose."

International institutions suffering from imbalance and inadequacy are creating a gap between the nature of the problems that need tackling and an institutional architecture primarily concerned with their own interests and enrichment.

Global governance is not "world governance". In fact, some believe that global governance would not be necessary, were there actually a world government in place. While sovereign nations currently have control of the use of force and the power of enforcement, that however, would be lost should a global or world government take over. This has been termed disaggregated sovereignty.

Improved global problem solving doesn't require the establishment of additional powerful global institutions; however, the elites want to use this approach as a means of furthering their agenda. For example, the UN Global Compact brings together companies, UN agencies, labor organizations, and civil society to support universal environmental and social principles. Whereas participation is voluntary, with no real enforcement or compliance, companies involved adhere to the practices because shareholders are able to look after their own interest while maintaining the appearance of concern for the citizens of the world. However, corporations who participate in the UN Global Compact have been criticized for their minimal efforts, the absence of sanction-and-control measures, and their lack of commitment to social and ecological standards.

One of the effects of globalization and global governance is the increasing numbers of rules placed upon businesses. Along with the growing globalization of social relations, has come an unprecedented expansion of regulatory apparatuses that cover global jurisdictions and constituencies. On the whole, however, global governance remains relatively weak. Shortfalls in moral standing, legal foundations, democratic credentials and charismatic leadership have together generated large legitimacy deficits in existing global regimes.

One of the conditions for building a world democratic governance should be the development of platforms for citizen dialog on the legal formulation of world governance and the harmonization of objectives.

This legal formulation could take the form of a Global Constitution, resulting from a process for the institution of a global community to act as the common reference for establishing the order of rights and duties applicable to United Nations agencies and to the other multilateral institutions, such as the International Monetary Fund, the World Bank, and the World Trade Organization.

As for formulating objectives, the necessary but insufficient ambition of the United Nations Millennium Development Goals, which aim to safeguard humankind and the planet, and the huge difficulties in implementing them, illustrates the inadequacy of initiatives that do not have popular support, having failed to invite citizens to take part in the elaboration process.

Furthermore, the Global Constitution must clearly express a limited number of overall objectives that are to be the basis of global governance and are to guide the common action of the U.N., agencies and the multilateral institutions, where the specific role of each of these is subordinated to the pursuit of these common objectives.

The following proposals have become the objectives of Global Governance:

1. Instituting the conditions for sustainable development.

2. Reducing inequalities.

3. Establishing lasting peace while encouraging; or more to the point, forcing diversity.

4. Reforming international institutions.

5. The security of societies through the need for global reforms by a controlled economy focused on stability, growth, full employment.

6. Equal rights for all through a global redistribution system.

7. Eradication of poverty in all countries.

8. Sustainable development on a global scale as an absolute imperative in political action at all levels.

9. Fight against the roots of terrorism and crime.

The question is: Is the UN capable of taking on the heavy responsibility of managing the planet's serious problems? More specifically, can the UN reform itself in such a way as to be able to meet the needs of the world? During the financial crisis of 2008, the same questions were posed, "Can international financial institutions be reformed in such a way as to provide swift financial help to countries in need?"

The answer is fraught with uncertainty. A distinct lack of political will and citizen involvement on an international level has brought about the submission of international institutions to the "neoliberal" agenda, particularly financial institutions such as the World Bank, the International Monetary Fund, and the World Trade Organization. Whereas the need for international institutions like the IMF, the World Bank, and the WTO has never been greater, people's trust in them has never been so low.

Radical reform of the UN has been advocated for years with such proposals being the building of new foundations which can provide the basis for a global democracy and the creation of a Global Social Contract. This contract would institute a new respect for the protection of civil, political, economic, social, and cultural rights, with an understanding of the strategic role of international law.

There are three 'gaps' in global governance which would require fixing before any type of governance can be successful.

1. There is an organizational gap between the alleged need for global governance in many

areas, such as health, security, and trade with the lack of a legislative body with the power to take action.

2. The gap of incentive between the need for international cooperation and the motivation to undertake it. The incentive gap is said to be closing as globalization provides an increasing push, through coercion if necessary, for countries to cooperate.

3. And lastly, the participation gap, meaning that international cooperation remains primarily the affair of governments, leaving civil society out in the cold when it comes to policy-making.

Initially, global governance was able to draw on the messages derived from geopolitics and the theory of international relations, such as peace, defense, diplomatic dealings, and trade relations. But as globalization progresses and with the increased inter-connection of agencies, the global initiative has become relevant to a far wider range of subjects. Below are a few examples:

Environmental governance and managing the planet brought about by the accelerated pace and the supposed irreversible effect of human activities on nature requires collective answers from governments and citizens. Nature doesn't care about political and social barriers therefore it cancels out any unilaterally action taken by state governments or institutions. Major culprits like climate change, ocean and air pollution, nuclear risks, increased reduction or extinction of natural resources, and even those caused by genetic manipulation remain largely self-evident, resulting in the afore mentioned acceleration and possibly irreversible effects of humanity on the environment.

There is some discussion on the possibility of setting up an international organization charged with centralizing all environmental protection issues, such as the proposed World Environment Organization (WEO) first discussed thirty years ago. The United Nations Environment Program (UNEP) could take on this role, but it is a small-scale organization with a limited mandate.

While the United Kingdom, the USA, and most developing countries prefer voluntary initiatives, the European Union, especially France and Germany, along with a number of other non-governmental organizations are in favor of creating a WEO.

Since 1992, the focus of environmental issues has shifted to climate change. Due to the nature of climate change, various calls have been made for the proposed WEO to tackle this global problem on a global scale, as a single worldwide governing body given powers to develop and enforce environmental policy. The WEO is again receiving renewed attention in light of disappointing outcomes from recent "environmental conferences" such as the Rio Summit and Earth Summit of 2002.

Many proposals for the creation of a WEO emerged from the trade and environmental debate. It has been argued that instead of creating a WEO to safeguard the environment, environmental issues should be directly incorporated into the World Trade Organization (WTO). The WTO has had success in integrating trade agreements and opening up markets because it is able to apply legal pressure to nation states in order to resolve disputes.

The creation of a new agency has been endorsed by the former head of the World Trade

Organization; however, the debate over a global institutional framework for environmental issues will undoubtedly trudge on as presently there is little support for any one proposal.

The 2008 financial crisis contradicted the myth that the all-powerful free-market forces will correct all serious financial breakdowns on their own. Far from being democratic and lacking in transparency, international financial institutions have proven incapable of handling another critical financial collapse.

The free-market economy is shown to be incapable of meeting the population's needs on its own. Without regulation and without consideration of social and environmental factors, free-market capitalism produces an uncontrollable machine that cultivates tremendous wealth in fewer hands, creating an elitist society of the wealthiest people on the planet. Its capacity to produce is not in doubt, but the problem is lack of fairness, perpetrated by the failure of our political figures to change the rules of the game to making it fair for everyone. The politicians (and Democrats more specifically) talk about inequality and injustice all the time, however none of them are willing to actually make the system fair. My guess is that

177

they have been gaming the system for so long that they don't want to give it up now, even if it means continued inequity among the lower classes.

Armed conflicts have changed in form and intensity since the 1989's collapse of the Berlin Wall. The events of 9/11, the wars in Afghanistan and in Iraq, and repeated terrorist attacks all show that conflicts can become lethal for the entire world, even when originating elsewhere. Many in the United States believe that fundamentalist Muslim networks, such as ISIS, are likely to continue to launch attacks, not just in America but all over the world. When the "Global War on Terrorism" emerged it could be argued that it represents a form of global governance in the name of security with the U.S. taking the lead among the Western coalition States. Participation in this form of 'harmonic governance' is caused both by a shared identity and ideology, as well as the sharing of cost considerations.

At the same time, civil wars continue to break out across the world, particularly in areas where human rights are not respected. These war torn regions remain deeply entrenched in permanent crises, hampered by authoritarian regimes, which reduce entire swaths of the population to living in wretched squalor.

The wars and conflicts we live within the 21st century are caused by a variety of factors, including economic inequality, Western imperialism, religious sectarianism, social conflict, disputes over territory and control of basic resources such as water, food or land; and most importantly, wealth.

The hostile climates lead to the creation of international collaborations with competitive nationalism and promotes, in rich and poor countries alike, the necessity for increased military budgets, draining huge resources of public money for the arms industry and military-oriented scientific innovation, fueling global insecurity.

Proposals for governance of peace, security, and conflict resolution must begin with preventing such conflicts in the first place. Whether they are derived from economic, social, religious, political, or territorial disputes, it will require the distribution of more resources so that the people affected can substantially improve their living conditions. Health, food, work, housing, and education especially in the areas of peace, social justice, unity, and diversity become two sides of the same coin representing "the global village".

Peace and security for successful global governing requires the implementation of global disarmament and the conversion of arms industries towards peaceful manufacture. (The Biblical beating of swords into plow-shares.) But to be successful, this must be applied equally to all countries, major powers included. Unfortunately, in the last decade, the warlike climate has served to designate all plans for global disarmament, even in civil-society debates, as a long-term goal or even a Utopian vision. This is definitely a setback for the cause of peace and for humankind, but it is far from being a permanent obstacle. Sooner or later we may have a world without nuclear weapons but with Obama's 2015 Iran Deal, that seems unlikely to happen. Experts predict that Iran will have weapons of mass destruction within a few years.

The Globalist agenda for advancing global security, peace and services as related to culture, science, education, health, humans, natural resources, information, and communication, have been partially offset by the anti-globalism movement. Globalist, to date, have been lacking political support but most of all, they lack widespread support of the citizenry. Without this support it will be impossible for them to obtain sufficient resources and alternative plans for society on a global scale will have to be proposed. In spite of the fact that numerous propositions and initiatives have been developed over the years, none of them were really successful at accomplishing the goals of the Globalist in their desire to build a fairer, more responsible and more solidarity-based Utopia which remained elusive.

The Foreign and domestic policy proposals announced by our two-term president, Barack Obama includes restoring the Global Poverty Act. This policy aims to reduce by half the world's population living on less than a dollar a day by 2015. Today in 2016, I found that the fund was officially closed and has essentially helped no one.

Foreign aid paid by the U.S. is expected to double to 50 billion dollars. The money will be used to help build educated and healthy communities, reduce poverty and improve the population's health in other parts of the world while doing nothing to help us here in the U.S.

In terms of international institutions, The White House Web site advocates reform of the

World Bank and the IMF, but failed to provide detail as to what their plans are.

Below are more points of interest in the Obama-Biden foreign policy plan that are directly related to the creation of global governance. I will let you decide on your own whether or not they have accomplished their agenda:

1. Strengthening of the nuclear non-proliferation treaty.

2. Global de-nuclearization in several stages including stepping up cooperation with Russia to significantly reduce stocks of nuclear arms in both countries.

3. Revision of the culture of secrecy, through the institution of a National Declassification Center to make declassification secure but routine, efficient, and cost-effective.

4. Increase in global funds for AIDS, TB and malaria. Eradication of malaria related deaths by 2015 by making medicines and mosquito nets far more widely available.

5. Increase in aid for children and maternal health as well as access to reproductive health-care programs.

6. Creation of a 2-billion-dollar global fund for education. Increased funds for providing access to drinking water and sanitation.

7. Other similarly large-scale measures covering agriculture, small and medium-sized enterprises and support for a model of international trade that fosters job creation and improves the quality of life in poor countries.

8. In terms of energy and global warming, Obama advocates a) an 80% reduction of greenhouse-gas emissions by 2050; b) investing 150 billion dollars in alternative energies over the next 10 years and; c) creating a Global Energy Forum capable of initiating a new generation of climate protocols.[6]

Citizen participation in decision making on a global level requires equality of opportunity to all citizens of the world.

Global democracy must guarantee that global public goods are equally accessible to all.

However, what I see happening is the strengthening of foreign governments at the expense of U.S. citizens. We don't need Global Governance, we need a nationalist government that works for everyone and is successful in serving the needs of our country.

Admittedly, some of the things presented in this chapter could, in a limited way, make the lives of the world's people better, but the same dynamic seems to occur over and over.

How is it that a person enters public service (probably with the best of intentions, at least in the beginning) making a modest salary and within several years ends up wealthy - a multi-millionaire?

Graft. They come to Washington and quickly become disillusioned with the pay for play, favors and positions are sold to the highest bidder. One of the most obvious example of this is when Congress voted to allow member of the House and Senate to participate legally in insider trading, a luxury that would land you or I in jail. Just ask Martha Stewart.

We have witnessed governmental corruption on an ever increasing scale and quite frankly, Americans have had enough.

"What makes the Universal Declaration an epochal document is first of all its global impetus and secondly the breadth of its claims, a commitment to a new social contract, binding on all the Governments of the world."

John Charles Polanyi

CHAPTER 6

WORLD GOVERNMENT

A World government is the concept of consolidating political control of all humanity, regardless of background, ethnicity or nationality. The idea would yield a global government that has legal authority over every living soul. Such a government could therefore exercise a world-wide martial law, based on events taking place around the world. Should an attack or other dispute happen on the other side of the globe, the global government would be able to lock down the rest of the world on a whim. In today's volatility, with the current daily terrorist acts taking place, this would be enough to force permanent compliance on the world as a whole.

Currently, the United Nations maintains a limited role and is merely an advisor. It's main purpose is to foster cooperation between existing national governments rather than exert authority over them. That will all change if Globalism becomes the law of the land.

Of course, the idea of world domination has been around since time immemorial; just recall Hadrian, Alexander The Great, Genghis Khan, Napoleon, and Hitler, to name but a few of the tyrants who have tried in the past. However, there has never been enough force behind it to actually implement it.

Humans by nature don't want to be controlled, they want to live their lives peacefully and by their own design, not by forced mandates of compliance by some little elitist oligarch on the other side of the world. Americans are especially protective of their freedoms, dating back to the Declaration of Independence. Their desire to maintain these freedoms extends beyond almost any other desire.

Allegedly, Globalist believe that a world government is essential in establishing world peace, yet I believe that their true goal through global governance is total control of the world.

Ayn Rand was correct when she said: "We are fast approaching the stage of ultimate inversion: the state where the government is free to do as it pleases, while the citizens may only act by permission".

In the mid 19th century, Ulysses S. Grant saw this coming when he stated, "I believe at some future day, the nations of the earth will agree on some sort of congress which will take cognizance of international questions of difficulty and whose decisions will be as binding as the decisions of the Supreme Court are upon us".

Grant obviously didn't fully understand at the time that the loss of freedom goes along with his forgone conclusion in the above statement is something that most people, not just Americans, will absolutely not tolerate.

In the early 19th century, international organizations began to form, with little notice on anyone's part as to their global design. With the establishment of the International Committee of the Red Cross in 1863, the Telegraphic Union in 1865, and the Universal Postal Union in 1874, came the first stepping stones on the path towards globalism and a world government. When I began researching this book, it shocked me as to just how many hundreds of years this idea of a global world really went back and furthermore, did they realize back then what they were actually proposing or how far current leadership would stray from the original design? The men and women who died for our freedoms would never tolerate what our current leadership is trying to do to those freedoms in the 21st Century.

With international trade increasing dramatically in the early 20th century, the creation of even more international organizations began to grow, with approximately 450 of them by World War I. Support for the idea of establishing international law grew during that period as well but failed to take hold. Globalists all through history have been pushing for a world government, but fortunately the will of the people has always been stronger. I am not sure that is still the case today, as we are closer to Globalism and a one world global government then we have ever been before.

During remarks in Omaha, Nebraska on June 5, 1948, U.S. President Harry S. Truman stated that: "We must make the United Nations continue to work, and to be a (on)going concern, to see that difficulties between nations may be settled just as we settle difficulties between States here in the United States. When Kansas and Colorado fall out over the waters in the Arkansas River, they don't go to war over it; they go to the Supreme Court of the United States, and the matter is settled in a just and honorable way. There is not a difficulty in the whole world that cannot be settled in exactly the same way in a world court". What we can take away from that is this: America's leaders have been pushing this world government idea for many decades and none of us paid enough attention to decipher exactly what they were proffering.

The years between the end of World War II and the start of the Korean War in 1950, the Cold War mentality became dominant in international politics. In Emery Reves' 1945 book "The Anatomy of Peace"[7] he laid out the argument for replacing the UN with a federal world government. Reves argued that "world law was the only way to prevent war, and the embryonic United Nations Security Council would be inadequate to preserve peace because it was an instrument of power, rather than an instrument of law." His publication quickly became known as the "bible" for the World Federalists Movement, established in 1947.

The World Federalist Movement is a global citizens movement. It advocates the establishment of a global federalist system of strengthened global institutions. They would have unconditional, yet constitutional power and international authority among separate global agencies. The organization was created by those concerned that the structure of the new United Nations was too similar to the League of Nations which had failed to prevent World War II. By 1950, the movement claimed 56 member groups in 22 countries, with some 156,000 members.

The movement never gathered much steam but were vocal nonetheless. They kept the idea of a world government alive and well in the hearts of those who wanted the power that came with it, a small core of activist and elitist. Eventually over time, the movement lost merit and the idea of a world government all but disappeared from public conversation.

However, the dissolution of the Soviet Union in 1991, brought the conversation of a federal world government and global protection of human rights back into the forefront. The world federalist took advantage of this opportunity and the movement's biggest achievement came in 1998 with the establishment of the Rome Statute of the International Criminal Court (ICC) which took effect in 2002.

The Rome Statute was successful in naming four international crimes as undeniable and punishable by the ICC. These were the crime of genocide, crimes against humanity, war crimes, and the crime of aggression; and these crimes were not subject to any statute of limitations. Under the Rome Statute, the ICC can only take action in these international crimes when states are "unable" or "unwilling" to do so themselves. Whether you view the establishment of the Statute as good or bad, it does brings us even closer to Global Governance and the New World Order.

Many organizations exist with the intention of creating a one world government. I have mentioned some of these earlier, like the IMF or WTO, but alarmingly, below are a few more current ones with that same end result, whether intentionally or not.

International agreements like the 1994 National American Free Trade agreement (NAFTA) signed into law by President Bill Clinton, or the Trans-Pacific Partnership (TPP) agreement signed by Obama in February 2016, (awaiting ratification by Congress) are global treaties and policies, legally binding by all parties involved. These treaties force partnerships with other nations like China, Japan, Mexico and most of the world in trade; but to date, the trade deals have not served America, but have worked out quite well for the other nations involved. Violations, particularly of trade agreements, which occur regularly by other nations against the U.S., are often intentionally overlooked and go unpunished.

The UN employs a military peacekeeping force whose duties range from rebuilding nations to maintaining peace and stability within a war-torn region. When a more aggressive action is necessary in order to obtain peace, the duty falls to a more qualified military alliance, such as NATO. The North Atlantic Treaty Organization is a military alliance of European and North American democracies founded after World War II to strengthen international ties between member states, especially the United States and Europe.

The International Criminal Police Organization or Interpol, is an international agency who facilitates international police cooperation. It was established as the International Criminal Police Commission (ICPC) in 1923 but in 1956, it became known as Interpol.

The G7 is an association of seven nations with the world's highest GDP or Gross Domestic Products. Their membership includes Canada,

France, Germany, Italy, Japan, the United Kingdom, and the United States. The G7 meet annually in person to establish and coordinate policies used to confront global issues, such as poverty, terrorism, infectious diseases, and climate change.

G20 is an international forum of governments and central bank governors from 20 major economies. Founded in 1999, its goal was to study, review, and promote high-level discussion of policy issues specifically pertaining to the financial stability of the world. Their members include: Argentina, Australia, Brazil, Canada, China, France, Germany, India, Indonesia, Italy, Japan, South Korea, Mexico, Russia, Saudi Arabia, South Africa, Turkey, the United Kingdom and the United States, and the European Union.

The European Union (EU) was established to unite politically a large group of nations. Though the EU is always evolving, it already has many characteristics of an growing federal government with policies such as open internal borders, an elected parliament, independent court system, and with the Euro being the official currency, they are able to establish a centralized monetary policy.

The European Union is said to have about 26% of the world's monies. Not all E.U. member states use the Euro. The United Kingdom, for example, still uses the pound, but the Euro provides easy circulation for trade of goods and resources. Tariffs are the same for each country, allowing no unfair practices within the E.U.. Just imagine how healthy the U.S. economy would be if we actually worked the same way and had across the board, fair and equitable trade like the rest of the world. The U.S. is about the only country on the planet that allows for such a deficit in trade to take place and of course, always to the detriment of America and American jobs.

America is drowning because of trade imbalances. Our debt in 2016 will quickly hit 20 trillion dollars, and that is not only a staggering amount but it is also catastrophic for the fiscal survival of our country. If this trend is not corrected soon, then the United States will be a much worse place for future generations to live in.

A United Nations Parliamentary Assembly (UNPA) was to be a component of the United Nations. It would have allowed for legislators of member nations, and possible citizens worldwide, to elect members to the United Nations. The idea was first raised in the 1920's with the founding of the League of Nations but was soon forgotten. It was suggested again at the end of World War II in 1945, but would again be tabled until the end of the Cold War. In the late 1990's and 2000's, calls for the Parliamentary Assembly began again in order to more closely scrutinize the activities of the UN. This renewed interest was caused by the dramatic rise in global trade and the power of world organizations. In 2007, the United Nations Parliamentary Assembly was officially formed, and as of July 2013 it has received the support of over 850 Members of Parliament from over 90 countries worldwide.

The Organization of Islamic Cooperation (OIC) is a group of 57 member states, all ranging from the Middle East, Africa, the Caucasus, Central Asia, Southeast Asia, the Balkans, and South Asia. This international organization now holds a permanent delegation within the United Nations, and claims it represents the Global Islamic World.

Since the 19th century, many Muslims have ramped up their attempts for the unification of a Muslim community with the purpose of serving their common beliefs.

The charter of the OIC aims specifically for the continued preservation of Islamic social and economic values through solidarity and cooperation amongst member states. It professes to increase cooperation in social, economic, cultural, scientific, and political areas; uphold international peace and security issues and advance education, particularly in the fields of science and technology.

If the intention of the OIC were as pure as they proclaim, then maybe, just maybe, we would not be seeing the attacks coming from the Islamic community that we have all become accustomed to seeing every day. This "charter" of the OIC does not sound like the agenda of the Muslims of the 21st century.

The ideology of the OIC seems sincere, claiming that everyone living is a creation of God, to be protected and encouraged as long as they are Muslim, worship Muhammad, live by the Quran and believe that the law of the land must be Sharia. As long as you follow their teachings, you will be spared. Everyone else has cause for concern.

The OIC adopted the Cairo Declaration on Human Rights in Islam on August 5, 1990. Their purpose was to guide member states in the matters of human rights. Though most of the world would find it laughable that Islam would even know what human rights are based on their treatment of women, gays and Christians, you have to remember one thing; In the mind of a Muslim, a human right must, and I stress must, be in compliance with the Sharia, or Quranic Law, anything less, is not acceptable to them. Can you say Allahu Akbar?

We hear that chanted at almost every major attack by Islam as they bomb, behead and slaughter innocent people. We heard it said at the "Pulse" nightclub on the night so many were gunned down by an Islamic Radical Terrorist. As gay people are thrown from the rooftop, women and children raped, we find that these these are the people Hillary Clinton wants to bring into our country by the millions.

With the increase of international trading, we soon became a "global market" as goods and services were now traded on an international level. Many people around the world began to see a visible improvement in their daily lives but we also created an inter-mingling amongst nations and world leaders, who along with exceedingly wealthy international corporations, could determine the activities of people worldwide.

The Internet, cable TV, GPS, and satellite "everything," made it possible for the news, information and public opinions to be available 24/7. Information is now free-flowing and instantaneous and we have found ourselves living in a much smaller world than we ever thought before.[8]

"We don't see the global citizen as someone with no identity, but rather someone who has confidence and is proud of his culture and history - and... open to the modern world."

Mozah bint Nasser Al Missned

CHAPTER 7

THE GLOBAL CITIZEN

A global citizen is simply someone who identifies more with the "global community" than any certain geographical region, like where you were born or where you live. The global citizen doesn't see a world with borders, they see a world-wide community; mankind being essentially one, in other words, a Global Community.

The global citizen will not waive their rights as citizens of an individual nation; however, in most cases, if not all, they will place the needs of the global community ahead of any loyalties that goes with "citizenship".

The education of our children is used as a method of spreading the concept of a global community into the minds of our young children. Educators and the Boards of Education, have been systematically removing or rewriting the learning materials to reflect not the pride one has for country but instead our children are taught tolerance for and acceptance of the global community. They are no longer taught "love of country", they are taught about global warming and that the world must be a world without borders. To the minds of our youth in 2016, the thoughts of a New World Order and global existence are not as scary to them as it is to older generations. They have been brought up believing that Socialism is not all that bad and they seem willing to give the global community a chance.

Within the departments of the educational system, global citizenship education is taking precedence over national education in some situations. Whereas most of us grew up learning about things "closer to home", the Millennials were aggressively taught how to live in a global community while abiding by the rules of globalism. Most millennials do become global citizens, believing that the needs of the environment and the community supersede the needs of the individual or the nation.

Global citizens accept a broad, cultural and environmental all-inclusive world-view that accepts the fundamental connection of all living things. Political geographic borders become irrelevant and solutions to today's challenges are seen as worldwide challenges without the interest of any individual nation considered.

If you asked a global citizen how they identified, they would tell you they are "citizens of the world, and the world is their family", never mentioning their nation of origin. The statement is not just about the bonding of whole societies, but also about a truth that somehow the whole world has to live together, as one family.

Psychological studies of those who believe they are global citizens, show that the ideology appeals most often to those individuals who share some strong personality traits. Those traits are an openness to experience, accepting of all things diverse, and they are largely agreeable people, empathetic and caring.

Not surprisingly, those who are strong in their belief of a global community are less prejudiced toward many groups. They are Social Justice Warriors caring about international human rights, worldwide inequality, poverty and human suffering. They share global concerns, valuing the lives of all humans equally, and give more in time and money to humanitarian groups. Politically, they tend to lean more left, having a liberal mind-set on both domestic and international issues. They believe countries should do more to stave off global suffering, yet they don't believe in the rights of a country to protect itself and its citizens.

At the same time that globalization is threatening the sovereignty of nations, the idea of global citizenship is gradually but increasingly pushing its way into main stream ideas. Face-to-face meetings have steadily been replaced by "virtual" meetings through video conferencing with no limitations on location and distance. We have become a global world and it no longer matters where on the planet you live - the world is at your fingertips.

The Internet gave us Social Media and then public opinion was heard the world over, shaping the discourse and shaping the world. For the Millennial, the rise of global citizenship has become the norm, indicating that they are willing to accept a global community; one they feel is more tolerant and inclusive. They have forgotten how it feels to have pride in one's nation, only feeling pride in the context of a global community.

The global citizen believes that all humans are born with inherent freedoms and do not discriminate based on race, color, sex, religion, or language. This protection also extends to one's political affiliations, nation of origin, social standing, or other such indicators of status. They believe in reason and an awareness that the "world is one" and they believe that everyone should be treated the same regardless of their actions or past indiscretions.

They believe in law and order but contend that global laws should carry more weight than national laws.

The global citizen is decent by nature, but also very naive. Whereas I agree that what they contend does have its appeal, it is naive in the fact that they are assuming everyone shares those values. The fact is, most of the world does not.

While the global citizen simply wants to live in a peaceful utopia and coupled with their willingness to live with a conformist mind-set, like sheep easily lead to slaughter, that has allowed globalism to sneak in and take hold; taking us prisoner, leaving us a dumbed-down generation, where "how one feels" is more important than "what is morally right".

In 2016, we witness a generation of people who accept and tolerate every alternative way of life imaginable and with that acceptance come a desensitization. The more they accept, the more extreme it gets and what we have now is a moral-less society where everything is acceptable as long as it makes you feel good.

Whereas the global citizen may one day prove to be an asset with their ability to reach around the world, right now we are facing a real enemy. It is not one that can be fought through the virtual world or by being complacent any longer.

Globalism has been promoted for hundreds of years but never before have we been this close to seeing it a reality. The wealthy industrialists, politicians and celebrities are drooling over the prospect of actually creating a New World Order; one that they control, and they have never been closer to achieving that than they are now. This is their last chance and they know it. Their last hope is in the form of a self-proclaimed Globalist, 2016 Democrat Presidential nominee, Hillary Rodham Clinton.

Today in 2016, if Hillary Clinton becomes the 45th President, the U.S. will find itself living in a Globalist World and the United Nations, controlled by the Elites, will have authority and global jurisdiction over everyone. And I mean EVERYONE.

"In almost every profession - whether it's law or journalism, finance or medicine or academia or running a small business - people rely on confidential communications to do their jobs. We count on the space of trust that confidentiality provides. When someone breaches that trust, we are all worse off for it."

Hillary Clinton

CHAPTER 8

HILLARY'S GLOBALISM

Globalism has given rise to extremely wealthy and powerful world-wide corporations and elites. The power that is held in the hands of so few is astounding. Individually, they all have their own strengths, but together their wealth rivals that of most nations. These are some of the richest people on the planet and they want to have control over you, your family, and everything about you.

Of the world's one hundred largest economies, almost half of them are multi-national corporations. Many of these are so large and wealthy that they easily dominate entire countries. Up to now they have been forging on in secret, but with the 2016 election, Globalism has been brought to the forefront. Hillary Clinton is no longer hiding the fact that she is a Globalist and her agenda for a Hillary Administration would yield our sovereignty to the United Nations. The elites and celebrities are following her lead and calling for Globalism as well, while they sit behind their gated mansions with security guards and guns.

President Obama and Hillary Clinton both believe in appeasing our enemies instead of standing up for our nation. Hillary Clinton would be a third term of Barack Obama and that is something, I personally, would not like to see.

As we face this election, the people of the world are beginning to see how devastating globalism can be. In 2016, the Presidential election is likely the most important one of our lifetime. I am a Baby-Boomer and I don't want to see the future of America under a Globalist regime, made up of the Elites and their chosen ones.

Hillary Clinton has broad reaching name recognition and she fully expects that the Presidency belongs to her. For most of her life, she has been working to secure her place in history. As Madame President, she plans to install an agenda that would place tremendous influence over our nation, politics, and politicians in the hands of regimes that have always maintained their hatred for Americans. With a President Hillary Clinton, the power of all nations will be in jeopardy, as she will fully allow The New World Order to be the law of the land.

According to an article written by Julia Hahn on July 14, 2016 for BreitBart News,[9] Hillary Clinton admits her plan for immigration far exceeds even those steps taken by President Obama.

Currently each year the U.S. admits one million plus foreign nationals (on green cards), one million guest workers, dependents, refugees, and half a million foreign students. In addition to the 1.5 million permanently resettled Muslim migrants that for more than a decade have already been allowed in, Hillary Clinton's stated proposal is that Muslim immigration will grow significantly under her than in previous years. She has stated that she will be adding nearly one million Muslim migrants to the U.S. population during her first term alone.

Even though it appears that the majority of immigrants, illegal or otherwise, are coming predominately from Muslim regions, using our porous borders from all directions, Clinton has said that she doesn't believe that is enough. As President, she indicated that she would expand Muslim migration by importing an additional

65,000 Syrian refugees into the United States during her first year in office.

She would grant them permanent asylum here in the U.S., essentially repopulating our country with millions of foreigners who don't understand our culture and don't respect our rule of law.[10]

Clinton's Syrian refugees would be an addition to the tens of thousands of Muslim refugees that the U.S. already grants entrance and a President Clinton has made no promises (not one you can believe anyway), that she would limit the numbers of Syrian refugees into the program each year to those numbers she gave the press.

If you add up Clinton's numbers, it means that in her first year, she will resettle approximately 215,000 Muslim migrants as President using her Syrian refugee program alone. Throughout her Presidency (without any increases) she will resettle more than 850,000 during her first term.

Once again, that is with no increase in applicants to the program; but as we all know from our brilliant and balanced government what we can expect to see are numbers that far exceed those that Clinton will admit to right now.

What really adds to those numbers are the relatives of migrants. Under Clinton's Syrian policy, once these migrants receive a U.S. green card they will have the ability to bring over their family members through chain migration.

Opposition to Clinton's Syrian Refugee plan is great but yet she won't reverse course. A September 2015 Rasmussen survey, published on Breitbart News, indicated that opposition to Clinton's Middle Eastern refugee plan by women voters was a remarkable 21-to-1 margin. Democrat voters oppose Clinton's refugee plan by a 17-to-1 margin. Most remarkably, 85 percent of black voters oppose Clinton's refugee agenda – with less than one percent of black voters supporting her plan.[11]

Yet Clinton's desire to flood our nation with Muslims, regardless of public opinion shows one thing very clearly. This woman is not in line with every-day citizens and voters. She lives in her ivory tower, with luxury and security and she thinks nothing about your family or your security.

Even worse are the possibilities beyond what she states. The U.S. Census data[12] shows that if a President Hillary Clinton were successful in passing a bill like the Gang of Eight immigration expansion bill, which eventually failed, the U.S. could permanently resettle roughly 9.4 million migrants throughout the nation during Hillary Clinton's first term in office. That gigantic figure doesn't even include the eleven million illegal immigrants already here that Hillary Clinton and her Vice Presidential hopeful Tim Kaine have promised amnesty and U.S. citizenship.

Clinton's desire to expand immigration is shared by GOP House Speaker Paul Ryan as well. Ryan claims to be one thing, but his voting records says something entirely different. Speaker Ryan has given President Obama a blank check through bloated budgets that somehow get through both chambers. We gave them control to stop the spending but instead they granted almost every Democrat request, from funding Obamacare, Planned Parenthood, and Obama's Executive Amnesty, to handing over more power to Obama so he can pursue his agenda without having to bother with that pesky Congress. After all, what have they proven to be good at? Allowing Obama to escape impeachment while handing him the nation's purse. Today's GOP has in most cases, folded to Obama at every turn.

Ryan has championed policies from expanding Muslim migration into the United States by refusing to fund the building of a wall to threatening to sue a President Trump (should there be one) if he tries to curb immigration and build a wall. The people of this country see Paul Ryan in a different light in 2016 than they did in past years. With this election and the open proposal of Globalism as well as the "coming out" so to speak with regards to who exactly the real globalist are, Ryan refuses to back down on any possibility of curbing Muslim immigration and has frequently chastised Donald Trump for advocating policies to reduce not only illegal immigration but also catching possible terrorist immigrants using the system to destroy our nation.

Paul Ryan's record shows that over a twenty year history he has continued to support an open borders immigration policy, even though, according to Pew polling data, 92% of GOP voters and 83% of American voters overall want to see immigration levels frozen or reduced,[13] as Donald Trump has suggested.

In spite of public opinion, (which is on Donald Trump's side on this issue), Ryan has continued his denouncement of Trump's immigration plan, even going so far as to use Democrat rhetoric in his efforts to discredit Trump's proposals.

In recent weeks, Ryan has come under fire in his home district in Wisconsin for continuing to vote to expand Islamic immigration, despite the fact that allegedly seven out of ten Wisconsin GOP voters would like a Muslim immigration pause.

Hillary Clinton and Paul Ryan seem to meet eye-to-eye on the issue of immigration, which makes a Clinton Presidency all the more worrisome.

Clinton's stated positions on the issue of immigration suggests that she holds the most extreme views on open borders and immigration as any candidate who has ever run for the office of the U.S. Presidency. Her views place her even further away from the mainstream views of the American electorate. Even more so than President Obama, a man who systematically dismantled U.S. immigration law during his two terms in office.

Below are just a few of the extreme immigration positions held by Clinton, as printed everywhere on the Internet. Mrs. Clinton has made it quite clear that these stated positions are indeed hers and that if she is elected president, she will implement every one of these policies and more, which will further her ideology and belief in the Global Government. Please read carefully, as these are her own words:

(1) Expanding Unconstitutional Executive Amnesty

Perhaps one of the most telling aspects of Clinton's campaign is her stance on open-borders and that she feels confident enough to openly campaign on this issue, even defending her plan to expand President Obama's unconstitutional executive amnesties. She has to know that this is against the wishes of most of the electorate, yet she expects to become president campaigning against the will of the people? Are there really that many people who will vote for her that she feels it is okay to ignore the voters? I guess Hillary Clinton thinks so.

She states, "You can count on me to defend President Obama's executive actions on DACA and DAPA when I am president," Clinton said, referring to Obama's 2012 (DACA) and 2014 (DAPA) executive amnesties, which gave work permits and access to federal benefits to millions of illegal immigrants.

She campaigns on expanding the government, she preaches about globalism, and she openly campaigns on the rights of the illegals who cross our border, unimpeded every day of the year.

(2) She has promised them: Amnesty Within 100 Days

Clinton has pledged to enact amnesty within her first 100 days in office and has made no secret that when she says "comprehensive immigration reform," she means full citizenship for illegal immigrants and migrants, which would give them welfare access, voting privileges, and the ability to take your jobs and your opportunities to achieve the "American Dream" for your family.

As a president, Hillary Clinton has stated that she will fight for a full and equal path to citizenship, regardless of method of arrival.

Now, one thing to keep in mind is that while Hillary Clinton is flooding our nation with Muslim immigrants; the Democrats, with Clinton, Obama, George Soros and the rest of the elites sitting behind armed guard security want to take away your gun rights. Hillary Clinton and her Vice President, Tim Kaine have made it their campaign promise to enact vast gun control through bans and eventually confiscation. A President Clinton will appoint several Supreme Court Justices in her first term and I can assure you that her choices will not put our Constitution first. They will enact a liberal agenda, including gun control and the abolishment of the Second Amendment,

While they are flooding our country with people who want to kill us, they are leaving us defenseless, with no way to protect ourselves. With the already high levels of crime coming from every direction, Hillary Clinton will leave us sitting ducks.

In 1970, fewer than one in 21 Americans were foreign-born. Today, as a result of the federal government's four-decade-long green card gusher, nearly one in seven U.S. residents was born in a foreign country. And in seven years time, according to Census Bureau reports, the foreign-born share of the U.S. population will reach an all-time high. Clinton's amnesty plans for the illegal immigrant population will cost U.S. taxpayers more than $6.3 trillion, according the Heritage Foundation report.

Clinton's pledge for amnesty perhaps explains why she won the endorsement of open borders advocate Luis Gutierrez, who has previously said "I have only one loyalty... and that's to the immigrant community." Gutierrez has been a strong advocate for illegal immigrants still crossing the border every day. He has made it his agenda to see that as many illegals from the South find a way to cross the border and step onto American soil. From there, they simple walk past our capable Border Patrol and pile into vehicles supplied by the Obama Administration and spread out through the United States with instructions on where to report in order to get the benefits that have always been reserved for citizens.

In return, Clinton praises Gutierrez, declaring that "few people have done as much as Luis to make sure that when it comes to America's policies on immigration, those policies reflect America's values. He organizes, strategizes, preaches, teaches, inspires, cajoles, whatever it takes to keep this movement moving forward."

Gutierrez doesn't know a thing about what it is like to be an American and he certainly should not have a voice in immigration since it is clear, his loyalty is not with America's laws but with her illegals.

Interestingly, Paul Ryan also won the early endorsement of Gutierrez prior to being elected as

House Speaker. It seems that Paul Ryan's views on foreign immigration, foreign trade, and foreign wars are more similar to Hillary Clinton's views than those of GOP nominee Donald Trump.

(3) Freezing Deportations

Clinton has said that, as President, she will essentially freeze all deportations.

"I would not deport children. I do not want to deport family members either," Clinton has declared and her pledge not to enforce current U.S. immigration laws as President, she takes a bold and unprecedented step toward a full open border society. This is a complete departure from our nation's history of enforcing immigration laws and is a slap in the face to struggling Americans across the nation.

Some of the most fervent Clinton supporters see her pledge as a tremendous step toward open borders but they push her to go even further.

Clinton's immigration policies will erase completely the protections that U.S. immigration laws afford to American citizens: such as protecting Americans from losing a job to an illegal immigrant, preventing the draining of school and hospital resources, as well as defending the voting privileges and rights given to U.S. citizens.

Clinton's has a stated platform that illegal entry is not in and of itself a deportable offense, which gives her wiggle-room when it comes to deportation. The administration also encourages millions of people to come here illegally, making it well know in parts of South American that all you have to do is make it to America and you will be welcome with open arms. Come, take our jobs, attend our U.S. schools, receive affirmative action, apply for federal benefits, and give birth to children who receive birthright citizenship. All they have to do is make it here and the goose that lays the golden egg is theirs for the taking.

We are all painfully aware that our immigration laws will not be enforced until after an American has been victimized, raped, or murdered by a criminal illegal. This federal guideline of waiting until after a crime has been convicted means that criminals are being allowed on our streets to roam free until they have committed a crime. They then have to be apprehended, tried, and convicted for that crime. After that, they are supposed to be deported, but as we have seen with the Obama administration, committing a crime, even rape or murder against an American Citizen is NOT a deportable offense, either. Clinton and Obama place the value of illegals leagues above the value of American Citizens.

(4) There's no need to secure the border because it's already "the most secure border we've ever had."

Even as tens of thousands of migrants pour across our southern border, Clinton declares that the border is "the most secure border we've ever had". This suggesting indicates that she does not feel it is necessary to take additional actions to secure our border. Clinton argues that since the border is already secure, it is time to give amnesty to the millions of migrants who have entered illegally.

"We have the most secure border we've ever had... The Republicans, the opponents, no longer have an argument," Clinton said during a March CNN/Univision Democratic debate. "We enhanced the border security. That part of the work is done... Everybody who I know who has looked at it says it is OK. We have a secure border. There's no need for this rhetoric and demagoguery that still is carried out on the Republican side. You've run out of excuses. Let's move to comprehensive immigration reform with a path to citizenship."

What planet does this moron Hillary Clinton live on? Can she not even make a pretense of listening to the people of this nation?

(5) Closing Detention Centers

On her website, Clinton pledges to end family detention centers by closing most of the privately run immigrant detention facilities".

Hillary believes we should "...end family detention for parents and children who arrive at our border in desperate situations. We have alternatives to detention for those who pose no flight or public safety risk, such as supervised release." Clinton's website explains, but as well know, when it comes to illegals, the government always manages to somehow, I don't know, "lose them."

This again represents a radical step in further dismantling what little immigration enforcement is now in place. Clinton is essentially saying that she will not detain new incoming illegal immigrants, but will instead release them into the streets of the United States.

(6) Obamacare for Illegal Aliens

Clinton has repeatedly said that she supports giving Obamacare to illegal immigrants. Clinton's website says that Clinton wants to "Expand access to affordable health care to all families... She believes we should let families--regardless of immigration status--buy into the Affordable Care Act exchanges".

Chelsea Clinton echoed this sentiment while campaigning for her mother. "It's so important to extend the Affordable Care Act to people who are living and working here, regardless of immigration status, regardless of citizenship status," Chelsea Clinton said in March.

With a nation that is currently bankrupt, who is going to pay for this Mrs. Clinton? YOU?

(7) Full Path to Citizenship

Clinton has pledged to use federal resources to ensure that millions more foreign migrants are able to vote in U.S. elections:

"There are millions of people in America who could be naturalized, but for one reason or another, they're not. So let's help more of our neighbors claim their rights. It's so powerful, so precious, to be a citizen of the United States!" Clinton said.

"To be able to vote in our elections, to have a voice in our future, and I want to take down the barriers that are holding people back. So here's a few things I will do: I will work to expand fee waivers, so more people seeking naturalization can get a break on the costs. I will increase access to language programs to help people boost their English proficiency. I will enhance outreach and education so more people know their options and are engaged in the process. I don't want anyone who could be a citizen to miss out on that opportunity".

Now come on Hillary Clinton, we all know that the only reason you are pandering to the illegals is because you want to turn them into your next bloc of slaves. Black America is waking up to you, so now you need the illegals to pull off your election theft.

Political scientists have documented how mass immigration helps Democratic politicians. As

University of Maryland's James Gimpel noted: "the enormous flow of legal immigrants into the country -- 29.5 million 1980 to 2012 -- has remade and continues to remake the nation's electorate in favor of the Democratic Party."

(8) Expanded Refugee Resettlement

Hillary Clinton has called for a massive expansion in Middle East migration. Oh, and that includes importing their diseases, as most of these migrants are not screened for infectious diseases before being placed in cities all over our nation. Vermont and Minnesota have already produced reports that indicated 32% of migrants brought in have latent Tuberculosis, yet they refuse to disclose how many have active TB. Measles is also on the rise in the U.S..

As Donald Trump has observed, Crooked Hillary wants a radical 550% increase in Syrian refugees and she declares to them that, "I'll work to ensure that every single refugee who seeks asylum in the United States has a fair chance to tell his or her story, this is the least we can offer people fleeing persecution and devastation," Clinton said in December.

231

Breitbart News previously reported below a more detailed breakdown of Islamic migration that would occur in Clinton's first term under the minimum numbers she has put forward to date:

374,000 refugees/asylum seekers from the Middle East during her first term, based on DHS data.

420,000 refugees/asylum seekers from the Muslim world during her first term.

560,000 permanent migrants from the Middle East during her first term.

730,000 permanent migrants from the Muslim world during her first term.[14]

Those numbers are staggering and the American people have had enough. More voters agree that we should limit the number of refugees from the Middle East if we are going to survive as a nation.

Hillary Clinton's plan for immigration will allow for the unfettered access of "Radial Islamic Terrorists" to descend on our country, bringing with them a religion of horror.

All of us have witnessed the horrors perpetrated by ISIS and other radical Islamists. It has become an everyday occurrence for some regions but all over the world we see the images of beheadings, slaughter of children, women stoned, people drowned in large cages or gays persecuted and killed. How long are we going to sit by waiting for this to happen in our country, to our families and to our children?

In stark contrast to Hillary Clinton's support for open borders, Donald Trump has called for a common sense "mainstream immigration policy that promotes American values."

"That is the choice I put before the American people: a mainstream immigration policy designed to benefit America, or Hillary Clinton's radical immigration policy designed to benefit politically-correct special interests." Trump said following the Orlando terrorist attack, wielded by the child of Afghan immigrant.

Trump continues, "Clinton wants to allow Radical Islamic terrorists to pour into our country-- they enslave women, and murder gays. I don't want them in our country. Immigration is a privilege, and we should not let anyone into this country who doesn't support our communities – all of our communities..." Trump went on to state, "The burden is on Hillary Clinton to tell us why she believes immigration from these dangerous countries should be increased without any effective system to screen who we are bringing in. The burden is on Hillary Clinton to tell us why we should admit anyone into our country who supports violence of any kind against gay and lesbian Americans. The burden is also on Hillary Clinton to tell us how she will pay for it. Her plan will cost Americans hundreds of billions of dollars long-term. Wouldn't this money be better spent on rebuilding America for our current population, including the many poor people already living here?"

America currently admits more immigrants than any other country and yet we continue to admit millions more with no real vetting. Not surprisingly, jobs and income have stagnated for years, so whether we call it a matter of national security, or a matter of financial security, we can't afford to keep on going like this.

The country owes $19 trillion in debt, and there are not many options left. All communities, from all parts of America need relief from the financial burdens they live under. Cities are broke, some filing bankruptcies. Our country's roads and bridges need massive repairs. We have to begin to think about America once again and anyone who loves this country should feel the same way. Obligations have to be reexamined to determine our priorities as a nation. Do we continue to take care of the world? Or do we start taking care of America first? No offense intended for anyone, it is simply an act of self-preservation.

On July 14, 2016, Clinton announced that if elected President, she will expand President Obama's illegal amnesty even further. The courts have so far blocked Obama and his lawless amnesty but that seems to carry no weight with Obama or Clinton.

Congress and the American people rejected the President's scheme of granting amnesty to those in the country illegally, and those who overstay their visas. Yet, Clinton recently said she would not deport anyone unless they commit a violent crime or if they are involved in terrorism. And, in a direct assault on the very foundations of our entire legal immigration system, she has boldly and radically vowed to go even further than President Obama.

Hillary Clinton will provide relief from deportation for those who are here illegally, but also provide employment authorization documents, photo IDs, Social Security numbers, the right to draw Social Security benefits, and the right to draw other state and local welfare and support payments - including Medicare for some. Where Obama failed to get his entire agenda passed, President Clinton has vowed to finish it for him. Like Obama, Hillary Clinton will use executive powers to enact whatever she wants to get done, bypassing Congress and the will of the people.

Hillary's Clintons commitment to the globalization of mankind is one hundred percent. She will stop at nothing to accomplish that goal. Yet she is not alone. Clinton has a powerful army of like-minded individuals, like her, who have power and money to get whatever they want. They are never affected by the chaos they create, they just sit back with their whiskey glass in one hand and a cigar in another and laugh over the power they picked up that day. Ruthless, driven wealthy men and women controlling the lives of everyone . "Conspiracy?" You say. Not at all.

An article written by Veronica Dagher, on Aug. 8, 2016 for the Wall Street Journal stated that the billionaires spread around the world number about 2500.[15]

These are the people who are pulling the strings. Hillary Clinton is somewhere on that list.

Today's elites is very different from what they used to be. This idea of a New World Order is by no means a new idea, as we discussed in earlier chapters, it has been around almost forever. But the 21st century elites have figured out how to actually turn their grand ideas of a Global World with only one established order, the elites. They are better organized, they have the Internet for recruiting and they have mastered the art of indoctrination with political propaganda served up to our smallest of children as soon as they enter kindergarten.

The elite have been planning this for a long time. They have advanced technology on their side, the best money can buy, and they are not afraid to use everything they have in order to ensure their dominance. These elitists seek a perfect utopia which include only them and their chosen ones. If we don't stop them, their utopia will be the enslavement for the rest of humanity, and the middle class, for decades to come. If the Globalists are successful, there will be no going back as they will eliminate those who do not serve a purpose and replace them with new improved genetically engineered servants, remember the Super-Computer?

The fact that Clinton has voiced her willingness to go even further than Obama in matters of immigration, should disqualify her for any position of authority within the Federal Government of the United States.

The American people overwhelmingly want a lawful immigration system that treats applicants fairly and serves the national interest. They are tired of illegal immigration and the failure of those immigrants to assimilate into our societies instead of forcing the society to change for them. They want to come to America but then they want to change everything about it. Americans are tired of paying for these people to live here. The tax payer is broke and yet they want even more money to pay for people who have no right to be here in the first place?

Democrats, like Clinton, have created roughly 340 sanctuary cities across America and four entire sanctuary states which are: California, Colorado, New Mexico and North Dakota. The sanctuary locations provide refuge for murderers, rapists, pedophiles, gang members, drug dealers, etc. Obama is releasing large numbers of these criminals into our communities rather than deporting them because they represent future voters for the Democrat party regardless of the danger they pose to our citizens.

Democrats and Republicans, like Paul Ryan, will continue to line their pockets with donor cash from special interests, big labor, & the Chamber of Commerce, all pushing for continued and even increased immigration to drive down wages. They are nothing but greedy and will sacrifice an American worker by providing incentives for companies to hire the migrant over the American. The underpaid foreigner takes your job and gets your benefits. As migrants are exempt from the Obamacare requirement of providing health insurance, and most Americans are not, these corporations can hire migrants and let them work 40 hours while the American is allowed to only work 30 hours a week. While Americans are watching their lives diminish, the migrant worker is thriving; thanks to taxpayer funded benefits like welfare, food stamps, free/subsidized housing, free educations, free health care, Obama-phones, etc.

Americans know that if Hillary is elected we will become the land of cheap imported labor with displaced and unemployed Americans living in poverty and forgotten. We will see our taxes increase to subsidize these new recipients while they cut Veteran and Elderly benefits to compensate.

The CBO has repeatedly told us that illegals are an unsustainable drain on our already weakened economy and that the immigrant family will receive more in taxpayer funded benefits over their lifetimes then they will ever pay in taxes. What budget can withstand that deficit? None, not for long anyway. Eventually our economy will come crashing down around us and the Great Depression will return once again.

Americans are sick and tired of the daily corruption, lies and demagoguery that takes place. Americans want civility, law and order and we don't want to press "1" for English any longer. We want to be treated like Americans again and not like we are third-rate citizens in our own country. If Clinton is elected, things will get so much worse.

How will a theoretical President Clinton pay for her immigration plans and welfare for all? She is going to dramatically raise taxes on everyone, especially the Middle Class.

Hillary Clinton has made clear she intends to dramatically raise taxes on the American people if elected. She has proposed an income tax increase, a business tax increase, a death tax increase, a capital gains tax increase, a tax on stock trading, an "Exit Tax" and more (see below). Her planned net tax increase on the American people is at least $1 trillion over ten years, based on her campaign's own figures.

According to American Tax Reform (atr.org),[16] Hillary has endorsed several tax increases on middle income Americans despite pledging not to raise taxes on working Americans making less than $250,000. She has said she would be fine with a payroll tax hike on all Americans and endorsed a 25% national gun tax, and most recently, her campaign manager John Podesta said she would be open to a carbon tax.

Hillary's proposed $1 trillion tax increase would be devastating to American families. On top of sky-rocketing Obamacare premiums, we can also expect some, if not all of the tax increases below, as part of a Clinton plan:

Income Tax Increase - $350 Billion: by capping the deductible portion of itemized deductions on your Income Tax Return to 28%, a Clinton Administration would generate the equivalent of a $350 billion income tax hike.

Business Tax Increase - $275 Billion: without disclosing hr intention of "how", Clinton has called for a tax hike of at least $275 billion through Business Tax Increases.

"Fairness" Tax Increase -- $400 Billion: According to her published plan, Clinton has called for a tax increase of "between $400 and $500 billion" by "restoring basic fairness to our tax code." These proposals include a "fair share surcharge," the taxing of carried interest capital gains as ordinary income, and a hike in the Death Tax.

Capital Gains Tax Increase - Clinton has proposed an increase in the capital gains tax. Her plan calls for a capital gains tax program with six different rates. Again, her campaign has no real details.

Tax on Stock Trading -- Clinton has proposed a new tax on stock trading. Costs associated with this new tax will be felt most by the millions of American families that hold 401(k)s, IRAs and other savings and retirement accounts. Like before, no dollar amount for this tax hike has been released by the Clinton campaign either.

"Exit Tax" – Rather than reduce the extremely high, uncompetitive corporate tax rate, Clinton has proposed a series of measures aimed at inversions including an "exit tax" on income earned overseas. The term "exit tax" is used by the campaign itself. Her campaign document describing this proposal says it will raise $80 billion in tax revenue, but claims some of the $80 billion will be plowed into tax relief. How much? The campaign doesn't say.[17]

Just as Hillary Clinton likes to portray Donald Trump as having "no substance" she fails in most cases to reveal anything about how she plans to pay for most of the things she wants to enact. Few details mean fewer questions for her. In addition to those mentioned above, the Clinton tax proposal will have more taxes to be announced later; you can be assured. Many experts believe that the Clinton net tax hike figure will likely be much higher than the already staggering $1 trillion dollar estimate.

Like Obama, a President Clinton will continue on a rampant path of tax and spend. Our country is bankrupt now and between her radically extreme immigration plans and the Hillary Clinton tax hikes, she will destroy what is left of the the Middle Class then she will be on her way to her Globalist Utopia.

Hillary Clinton is a danger to our country and our children's futures in so many ways. Those die-hard anti-Trump Republicans who are willing to thwart the people by placing their support with either Clinton or sitting at home, are just as complicit as she is. Anyone who doesn't participate will be directly responsible for electing a President who seeks to bring about the complete, and possibly irreversible, dissolution of our Constitution. A president who will walk us down the path to globalism and deny us our national sovereignty.

"Those who make peaceful revolution impossible will make violent revolution inevitable."

John F. Kennedy

CHAPTER 9

BREXIT

Not only is the United States having to come to terms with the globalist agenda, but the entire world is beginning to feel themselves pulled in that same direction and some are fighting back.

Countries like Germany, France, Italy, Sweden and Great Britain have all seen an influx of migrants flooding their borders. With the migrants comes crime: robbery, assault, rape, and even murder. Under the control of Angela Merkel, Chancellor of Germany since 2005, Germany has, like so many other areas, been turned into a play ground for the migrants. They harass women and girls while complaining about food and their accommodations. They are turning large portions of Europe into a chaotic mess, leaving behind filth, trash and broken people in their wake. The Muslim migration has become a serious issue and as the Internet photo's show, they are mostly men and they are wrecking havoc on any town they descend upon. They are moving swiftly and little by little, the Islamic community is taking over parts of the world.

They say that Barack Obama and Hillary Clinton created ISIS and I guess that is a debate for another day, but if that is true, then those two have unleashed on the world a horror like most of us have never seen. Our lives of civility have been tested on a daily basis and people are beginning to see that their governments are indeed working against them. It hardly seems possible but it is true. The United States government in 2016 is selling the country to the highest bidder and Hillary Clinton wants to head the negotiations through the Office of the Presidency.

Around the world, the signs of globalism are growing and we are quickly approaching the proverbial fork in the road. Do we go left and straight to globalism or do we go right, and remain America. There is no way to do both.

2016 is the Year of the Globalist as we have watched many world leaders stand up and proclaim their globalist intentions. They don't even try to hide it any longer. The rich and powerful believe that if they can get Hillary Clinton elected, keep her alive long enough to sign a few documents, then they won't need the old lady any more. Hillary Clinton is merely a pawn, expendable like the rest of us, in the elite's race to the prize - their perceived place at the top of the world.

It took a brave country, Great Britain, to show us that if we take a stand, we may prevail. They did, and against all odds. Prime Minister David Cameron didn't see the loss coming when he opened his country up to the promised referendum vote. Would the electorate of Great Britain vote to remain as members of the European Union or were they going to take their sovereignty back, sever their ties with the EU and become independent once again? This vote became known around the world as "Brexit" or Britain's Exit.

The elites, through George Soros, promised us the end of the world if Britain left the EU. They said Brexit would cause the financial collapse of the world economy. They were wrong; sure, the markets roiled for a few days but they settled out and nothing much happened. The sky didn't fall.

With their national vote, Great Britain voted to exit the European Union and become a sovereign entity again. They fought back against globalism and the never-ending forced migration thrust upon them through membership in the

European Union. The vote was watched the world over, as the countrymen and women of Great Britain decided the course for their lives. Which would it be?

And in the end, the patriotic people of Great Britain voted for Queen and Country in a vote for Nationalism.

Prime Minister David Cameron was forced to resign in a crushing defeat.

What we can take away from the Brexit vote is this: we are seeing the first signs of a chink in the armor of globalism. The people of Europe and all over the world watched Great Britain rise up. They slammed the door shut on globalism and big government with open borders and no immigration policy, and they proclaimed their nation sovereign again. The world was proud of Great Britain. Since then, other oppressed European nations have decided to have their own "exit" votes in the future and hopefully, one by one, globalism in Europe will fail.

The impact of Globalism is not the only reason Great Britain took a vote. It was the migrant issue, too. The over-whelming numbers of migrants were shocking but then the people realized that their government was going to allow this migration to continue to grow and conquer all areas it touches. This knowledge was too much to bear for many people. Citizens of once grand and beautiful countries were being forced to idly watch as their countryside was infiltrated with migrants who had no intention of assimilating but instead, dominating. Many innocent people were hurt and killed because of the Muslim migration that has swept Europe and is spreading throughout the world but the governments don't care. They are working towards an end-game and for them, the end justifies the means. You ask yourself "Why the sudden movement of so many young, healthy male migrants from the Middle East? Where are the women and children?" They claim to be refugees from Syria but in actuality, very few of them are even Syrian. They are principally from Afghanistan and Somalia; but they are also Iraqi, Pakistani, Libyan, and others.

I read an article recently about a migrant in France, relocated from the Middle East. He was quoted as saying. "We hate your country. We just want to **** your French women." Horrible and yet this is not an isolated incident, this is happening all over Europe. This is now the new reality and this is what the globalists want to import to America.

Hillary Clinton, President Barack Obama, George Soros, David Cameron, Chancellor Angela Merkel, and many other leaders of many other countries have intentionally allowed ISIS to prosper and it is fact that the U.S. is arming them and supplying them with money.

Liberals expect Clinton to win the Presidency; not win exactly, but be "given" by the small group of elites who make the rules. Hillary Clinton is small potatoes in the overall scheme of things. They will allow her to win, but they won't allow her to govern. The puppet masters will take over once she signs America over to the control of the UN.

You can't put the genie back in the bottle and if we allow Hillary Clinton and her Globalist buddies to take over the world, we are all in eminent danger. Hillary Clinton will continue to allow Muslim proliferation of our country because she knows that her family will be taken care of under The New World Order. Like Angela Merkel, who ruined Germany with open borders and over-whelming male Muslim immigrants, she will watch as the world is destroyed while she sits on her throne with the rest of the elites, like sick little gods, playing with the pieces on a chess board.

As more and more people become aware of the true nature of Globalism and where it leads, they realize that this may not align with where they want to go. Choices have consequences and this one has huge consequences for generations to come.

You have read the history and understand what globalism means now, so the next step is to determine your desired path of action. Do you want to relinquish our national sovereignty to the UN or do we fight the powers and the elites and restore our sovereignty. Do we fall victim to the rich and powerful and play their globalist games or do we kick them to the curb and tell them that we will not listen to them anymore. We want a secure border, jobs, and a strong economy. We want pride in our Nation. We want to be Nationalist.

I was going to stop Part 1 on this note, but the question nagging at me is this, "Who are these elites that are in control? How many of them are there and do they really control everything that happens, like some people believe they do. While doing research, I found what I was looking for.

"We must recognize that as the dominant power in the world we have a special responsibility. In addition to protecting our national interests, we must take the leadership in protecting the common interests of humanity."

George Soros

CHAPTER 10

GEORGE SOROS

The name George Soros is one that strikes fear in the hearts of those who know who he is. Soros is one of the biggest monsters on the planet and has the power to send grown men screaming into the streets. Like the other elites, Soros is fabulously wealthy but what makes him different is the hate he carries in his heart. Soros is a man who could run over a puppy in the road and laugh out loud when he feels the "bump" of the tires and hears the last squeal of the defenseless animal.

George Soros was Hungarian born in 1930 to a non-practicing Jewish family. He was thirteen years old when the Nazis occupied Hungary in March of 1944 and being Jewish, Soros and his friends were not allowed to attend school. They reported instead to the Jewish Council for small job assignments. He was eventually able to get into college and graduated with an impressive resume.

The young George has seen and survived many things from war to poverty but he learned a great deal, too. After graduating from college jobs were scarce but Soros had a capacity for seeing the big picture and decided that his destiny was not being a salesman of fancy-goods at Welsh seaside resorts; his destiny was in the financial markets. He began to solicit a job from every managing director in every merchant bank in London. After receiving only a couple responses, Soros took an entry-level position for the merchant bank, Singer & Friedlander and thus began his rise in the financial world. By the time Soros was 37, he had opened his own offshore investment firm and at 39, he opened his first hedge fund. By the time he turned 40, George Soros founded Soros Funds Management which ultimately grew into the enormous mega-fortune it is today.

George Soros is impressive in his unwavering determination and internal drive that delivered this young, poverty-ridden boy to become one of the wealthiest men on the planet.

Soros is well known for his financial wheeling and dealing. He even managed to make a $1 Billion dollar profit on a short sale of $10 billion (US) worth of British Pounds during the 1992 Black Wednesday UK currency crisis which afforded him the title of "The Man Who Broke the

Bank of England." While everyone else was losing money, Soros came out smelling like a rose.

Today, he is an old man of 86 years-old. He is many things from businessman, investor, philanthropist, political activist to an author who holds dual citizenship in Hungary and the United States. He is still the chairman of Soros Fund Management and currently holds the title of one of the "thirty richest people in the world" which provides him with power unimaginable to most of us. But at some point, George Soros decided to go down a dark path.

As a former Nazi collaborator, George Soros did and saw unimaginable and heinous things and in his young mind, he took it in and it became his path to walk. He grew to be so cold, callous, and he'd lost so much of himself that he thinks nothing of standing by and watching as humanity destroys each other.

There has never been a time in our history when we have been more divided as a country and agitators like Soros, Al Sharpton, and other organized groups, take full advantage of this division.

George Soros has admitted to being the chief organizer and funder of many directives that are designed to undermine humanity, such as The New Black Panthers, Black Lives Matters, the ACLU, the Occupy Wall Street movement, and the world-wide Muslim immigration.

In 2004, George Soros donated roughly 25 million dollars to organizations dedicated to defeating the re-election bid of President George W. Bush. In spite of their failure, Soros didn't stop. Failure only made him more determined.[18]

In 2010 Soros donated $1 million dollars in support of Proposition 19 in California. This bill would have legalized marijuana in the state and Soros really wanted it to pass. When it failed, Soros and a few other donors put their political power behind a fund-raising group called Democracy Alliance.[19] This new group was steadfast in its support of progressive causes; wanting a stronger more progressive infrastructure for America.

Soros was a donor to the Center American Progress, which was instrumental in the election of Barack Obama. Soros continues to support them through his Open Society Foundations, which currently have active programs in more than 60 countries around the world.[20]

For the most part, Soros has been maintaining a low-profile when it comes to his goal of Globalism but with the entrance of Donald Trump into the 2016 election cycle and the real possibility of a Trump win, Soros and the others find they are now in a "do or die" situation. Their time for globalism is now or never so instead of keeping a low profile, the globalists of the world are speaking out and hoping that they will sway enough votes to ensure a Hillary Clinton win so they can finish what they started.

George Soros is not the biggest player but he is one of them and in a recent interview published on Breitbart,[21] Soros admitted to be the driving force behind the Muslim migration around the world.

His main goal is to bring down all the borders in Europe, and eventually America, and provide protection for refugees subjugating the protection and safety of the nation and its citizens.

Soros is a firm backer of transnational bodies such as the European Union, and through his Open Society Foundation (OSF), he provides assistance to groups who share his open borders, pro-immigration ideology.

Black Lives Matters (BLM) is a group of disgruntled black Americans who have had enough of their perception of the treatment of Black America and have taken to fighting back against society. Until recently, we believed them to be nothing more than inner city blacks looking to stir up a little commotion but since they have begun popping up in cities in Europe, causing trouble and riots, we are asking "Who is financing them?" Well George Soros, that's who.[22]

Many of Soros' funded organizations are known to funnel money to dissident groups that create chaos, further escalating the anti-American, anti-police narrative in an effort to cause mass riots and destruction.

Soros will continue to encourage and fund the mass Muslim immigration movement throughout the world because what does it matter to him if many lose their lives along the way.

The Globalist knows that there will be collateral damage but they see this as acceptable because to them, the ends justify the means. In order for globalism to work, there must be no borders anywhere in the world. Just yesterday, ISIS boiled four men alive in hot tar. So yeah, those are really the people I want living with my family.

From what I am seeing, Soros and the other elites are allowing the Muslim movement to take over entire countries and regions, doing very little to stop them. ISIS will go about the business of killing everyone who is gay, white and Christian, while George Soros, Barack Obama, and Hillary Clinton sit on their hands, pretending not to notice the carnage by either ignoring it or calling them the "JV Team". My question to the three of them is this, "What are you going to do with the Muslims once they have done your dirty work for you?"

The elites are a bit naive if they think they can control the Muslims. I hope to be alive the day that they realize they are living in a world surrounded by hate driven Muslims. How long do you think it will take the Muslims to find them and exterminate them, too? The Muslims will never allow a group of infidels to live. It should be an interesting time, I would think.

George Soros is one of those men that rational people have said needs to die in order for the world to heal but it will take more than a Soros death to save humanity from his scorn. George Soros truly despises humans and believes he is above everyone. He has spent his life and a great deal of money buying everything he wants, including people. He has no morals and no concern for anyone outside of his fellow friends, thugs and cretins and Soros would sooner see you dead as opposed to being forced to deal with you in any way. The world will exhale when Soros dies, but the man reproduced and his son, Alexander Soros, is busy taking his father's place at the helm and having dinner dates with Hillary Clinton's right hand man and Vice Presidential candidate, Tim Kaine. Alex Soros posted this to his Instagram account:

"Love this man!" Alex Soros wrote along with a photograph of him with the vice presidential hopeful. "Was great to have dinner with a man we need to call one day #vicepresident @timkaine last night! He is definitely the real deal!"

Now what could those two possibly have to be so chummy about?

Soros' legacy will live on, way past his death and unfortunately, it may take generations for the Soros' influence and power to be spent. Soros' admission to funding and being the "mastermind" behind the Muslim immigration that has devastated

Europe and will soon find its way to America, shows us how evil this man has become. He cares nothing about you or America or the world and Hillary Clinton cares nothing about you, either.

Soros and Clinton both are so disturbed that they will watch people be killed by the policies they support and fund. If there is a policy, a group, a commission or just a bunch of thug activists, like BLM, set up to instigate trouble and chaos for humans, you can rest assured, George Soros has his money and his hands all over it somehow.

But like Hillary Clinton, George Soros is also a puppet. Like Clinton, Soros also has a puppet master. Even though he seems scary, rich and powerful, he is nothing more than a man on a string, doing what he is told to do by those even higher up. Soros is an abomination, but he is not the worst of them. George Soros also takes his orders from others.

"The very word 'secrecy' is repugnant in a free and open society; and we are as a people inherently and historically opposed to secret societies, to secret oaths, and to secret proceedings."

John F. Kennedy

KIMBERLY BRATTON

CHAPTER 11

THE BILDERBERG GROUP

There is one group of elites that we haven't touched on yet and they are a dangerous bunch. Some of us have heard about them and like the Illuminati's, we never gave them much thought. We believed them to be a hoax of sorts, just something conspiracy theorists like to say to scare little kids before bedtime. But this group does exist and they are working overtime to turn our world into their utopian horror.

Who are the Bilderbergs?[23]

The Bilderbergs are a group of highly wealthy and influential people whose entanglements spread around the globe many times over. They control behind the scenes some of the largest banks and corporations in the world and they pretty much get whatever they want. They meet once a year in secret to discuss world events, even keeping their meeting places private until the last minute. Attendance is by invitation only and if anyone slips or lets it be known that they were invited, then that person could be removed from the list and uninvited right away.

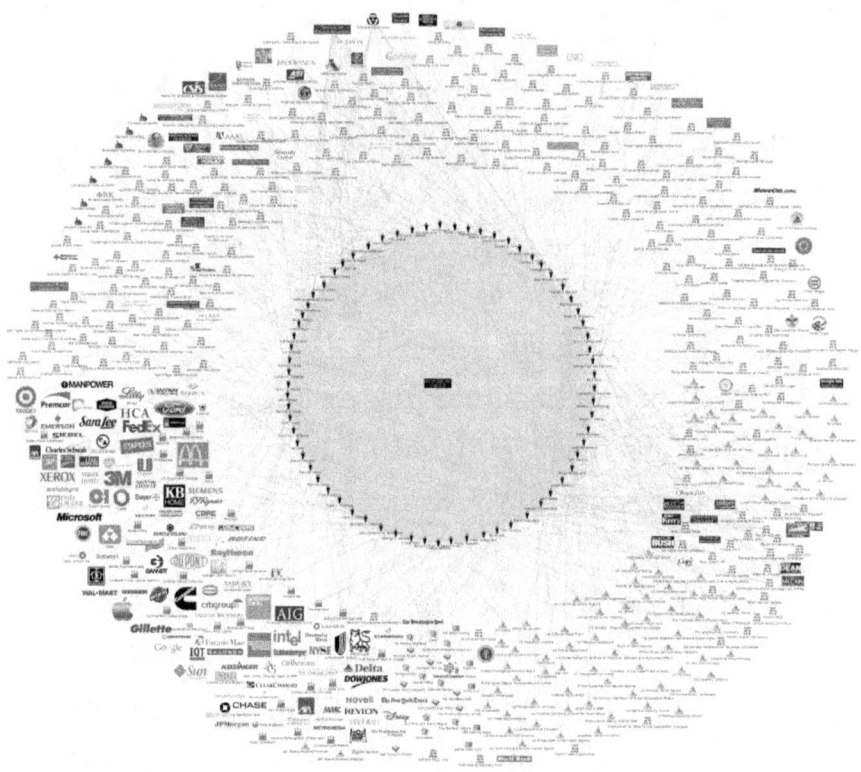

The diagram above[24] is an illustration of just how far the Bilderberg Group's tentacles reach. You have the Bilderberg Group in the center surrounded by the names in black of those attending the meetings. The outside group consists of representatives from every economic industry. The top represents the Medical and Academia world with the Kennedy Center, the Brookings Institute, Harvard and Princeton. The bottom left contains every government agency, commissions and group and some major politicians, like Mitt Romney, Hillary Clinton, Barack Obama, Joe Lieberman, John McCain and many more. Almost every major retail establishment and bank are represented along with major print, news groups, journalists, and celebrities.

Most of the tentacles on the diagram lead from the Bilderbergs out to the appropriate person or commission. Some eventually lead back to either the Council on Foreign Relations or the Trilateral Commission, at the top of the diagram. They have a perfectly woven inter-connected society of the world's elites, safely hidden behind the name Bilderberg.

The diagram is small and the integration between the groups is astonishing. I recommend you take a look at the link in order to view the diagram in its entirety. The link to the diagram is:

http://verdenken.blogspot.com/2014/04/anon
ymous-der-club-der-bilderberger.html

There has been many things written about the Bilderberg Group over the years, but most of it is shrouded in secrecy. Unless you are on the list, you really know very little about them. The Internet has changed that somewhat as information spreads across the globe, and today we know that the Bilderbergs consist of invited members only. Some people believe that the Bilderberg group is the one controlling the purse strings of the world and things only happen because they set them in motion. Some believe that these are the Leaders of The New World Order. Bill Clinton attends those meetings with George Soros, Melinda Gates, Ben Bernanke, Dianne Feinstein, William F. Buckley; who died in 2008, the Rockefellers and many more. The Rothschild Family and The Bank of England are at the top of the pecking order controlling The Federal Reserve Banks through stock-holdings. Ultimately, these people wield tremendous power.

As early as 1977, members of the Bilderberg group were seen as the richest, most influential people in both the economic and political world.

Discretion is a must for the group and to facilitate that, according to the group's code these meetings are intended to produce, "...no desired outcome, no minutes are taken and no report is written. Furthermore, no resolutions are proposed, no votes are taken, and no policy statements are issued."

The Bilderberg group also contains members of the Council on Foreign Affairs and the Trilateral Commission, even though their names may not appear on the main lists, they still work together to achieve their goal - the New World Order.

The elites believe that the planet can't sustain itself much longer, with population growth and less food resources, they expect that life will have to be altered dramatically in order for humans to survive.

Those at the center of that diagram are not afraid to make the necessary choices, that in their view, will save humanity, through survival of the fittest.

Former British Defense Minister Denis Healey, put it this way, "World events do not occur by accident. They are made to happen, whether it is to do with national issues or commerce; and most of them are staged and managed by those

273

who hold the purse strings.[25]" Meaning, the Bilderberg Group.

Every US president since Eisenhower has either belonged to the Bilderberg Group or was approved by the Council on Foreign Relations (CFR).

The 64th Bilderberg conference took place June 9-12, 2016 somewhere in Dresden, Germany. Approximately 130 participants from 20 countries confirmed their attendance at the event. As ever, a diverse group of political leaders and experts from industry, finance, academia and the media were invited. Some of these names you will recognize but most, you will not. Angela Merkel doesn't appear on the list, yet she was in attendance. High profile politically sensitive attendees are sometimes kept secret for security reasons. The list of participants is available on www.bilderbergmeetings.org.

The key topics for discussion for the 2016 Meeting will include:

1. Current events.
2. China.

3. Europe: migration, growth, reform, vision, unity.

4. Middle East.

5. Russia.

6. US political landscape, economy: growth, debt, reform.

7. Cyber security.

8. Geo-politics of energy and commodity prices.

9. Precariat and middle class.

10. Technological innovation.

Although this list may have been updated since publication, the final list of Participants to date, includes:[26]

Chairman: Castries, Henri de (FRA), Chairman and CEO, AXA Group

Aboutaleb, Ahmed (NLD), Mayor, City of Rotterdam

Achleitner, Paul M. (DEU), Chairman of the Supervisory Board, Deutsche Bank AG

Agius, Marcus (GBR), Chairman, PA Consulting Group

Ahrenkiel, Thomas (DNK), Permanent Secretary, Ministry of Defence

Albuquerque, Maria Luís (PRT), Former Minister of Finance; MP, Social Democratic Party

Alierta, César (ESP), Executive Chairman and CEO, Telefónica

Altman, Roger C. (USA), Executive Chairman, Evercore

Altman, Sam (USA), President, Y Combinator

Andersson, Magdalena (SWE), Minister of Finance

Applebaum, Anne (USA), Columnist Washington Post; Director of the Transitions Forum, Legatum Institute

Apunen, Matti (FIN), Director, Finnish Business and Policy Forum EVA

Aydin-Düzgit, Senem (TUR), Associate Professor and Jean Monnet Chair, Istanbul Bilgi University

Barbizet, Patricia (FRA), CEO, Artemis

Barroso, José M. Durão (PRT), Former President of the European Commission

Baverez, Nicolas (FRA), Partner, Gibson, Dunn & Crutcher

Bengio, Yoshua (CAN), Professor in Computer Science and Operations Research, University of Montreal

Benko, René (AUT), Founder and Chairman of the Advisory Board, SIGNA Holding GmbH

Bernabè, Franco (ITA), Chairman, CartaSi S.p.A.

Beurden, Ben van (NLD), CEO, Royal Dutch Shell plc

Blanchard, Olivier (FRA), Fred Bergsten Senior Fellow, Peterson Institute

Botín, Ana P. (ESP), Executive Chairman, Banco Santander

Brandtzæg, Svein Richard (NOR), President and CEO, Norsk Hydro ASA

Breedlove, Philip M. (INT), Former Supreme Allied Commander Europe

Brende, Børge (NOR), Minister of Foreign Affairs

Burns, William J. (USA), President, Carnegie Endowment for International Peace

Cebrián, Juan Luis (ESP), Executive Chairman, PRISA and El País

Charpentier, Emmanuelle (FRA), Director, Max Planck Institute for Infection Biology

Coeuré, Benoît (INT), Member of the Executive Board, European Central Bank

Costamagna, Claudio (ITA), Chairman, Cassa Depositi e Prestiti S.p.A.

Cote, David M. (USA), Chairman and CEO, Honeywell

Cryan, John (DEU), CEO, Deutsche Bank AG

Dassù, Marta (ITA), Senior Director, European Affairs, Aspen Institute

Dijksma, Sharon A.M. (NLD), Minister for the Environment

Döpfner, Mathias (DEU), CEO, Axel Springer SE

Dudley, Robert (GBR), Group Chief Executive, BP plc

Dyvig, Christian (DNK), Chairman, Kompan

Ebeling, Thomas (DEU), CEO, ProSiebenSat.1

Elkann, John (ITA), Chairman and CEO, EXOR; Chairman, Fiat Chrysler Automobiles

Enders, Thomas (DEU), CEO, Airbus Group

Engel, Richard (USA), Chief Foreign Correspondent, NBC News

Fabius, Laurent (FRA), President, Constitutional Council

Federspiel, Ulrik (DNK), Group Executive, Haldor Topsøe A/S

Ferguson, Jr., Roger W. (USA), President and CEO, TIAA

Ferguson, Niall (USA), Professor of History, Harvard University

Flint, Douglas J. (GBR), Group Chairman, HSBC Holdings plc

Garicano, Luis (ESP), Professor of Economics, LSE; Senior Advisor to Ciudadanos

Georgieva, Kristalina (INT), Vice President, European Commission

Gernelle, Etienne (FRA), Editorial Director, Le Point

Gomes da Silva, Carlos (PRT), Vice Chairman and CEO, Galp Energia

Goodman, Helen (GBR), MP, Labour Party

Goulard, Sylvie (INT), Member of the European Parliament

Graham, Lindsey (USA), Senator

Grillo, Ulrich (DEU), Chairman, Grillo-Werke AG; President, Bundesverband der Deutschen Industrie

Gruber, Lilli (ITA), Editor-in-Chief and Anchor "Otto e mezzo", La7 TV

Hadfield, Chris (CAN), Colonel, Astronaut

Halberstadt, Victor (NLD), Professor of Economics, Leiden University

Harding, Dido (GBR), CEO, TalkTalk Telecom Group plc

Hassabis, Demis (GBR), Co-Founder and CEO, DeepMind

Hobson, Mellody (USA), President, Ariel Investment, LLC

Hoffman, Reid (USA), Co-Founder and Executive Chairman, LinkedIn

Höttges, Timotheus (DEU), CEO, Deutsche Telekom AG

Jacobs, Kenneth M. (USA), Chairman and CEO, Lazard

Jäkel, Julia (DEU), CEO, Gruner + Jahr

Johnson, James A. (USA), Chairman, Johnson Capital Partners

Jonsson, Conni (SWE), Founder and Chairman, EQT

Jordan, Jr., Vernon E. (USA), Senior Managing Director, Lazard Frères & Co. LLC

Kaeser, Joe (DEU), President and CEO, Siemens AG

Karp, Alex (USA), CEO, Palantir Technologies

Kengeter, Carsten (DEU), CEO, Deutsche Börse AG

Kerr, John (GBR), Deputy Chairman, Scottish Power

Kherbache, Yasmine (BEL), MP, Flemish Parliament

Kissinger, Henry A. (USA), Chairman, Kissinger Associates, Inc.

Kleinfeld, Klaus (USA), Chairman and CEO, Alcoa

Kravis, Henry R. (USA), Co-Chairman and Co-CEO, Kohlberg Kravis Roberts & Co.

Kravis, Marie-Josée (USA), Senior Fellow, Hudson Institute

Kudelski, André (CHE), Chairman and CEO, Kudelski Group

Lagarde, Christine (INT), Managing Director, International Monetary Fund

Levin, Richard (USA), CEO, Coursera

Leyen, Ursula von der (DEU), Minister of Defence

Leysen, Thomas (BEL), Chairman, KBC Group

Logothetis, George (GRC), Chairman and CEO, Libra Group

Maizière, Thomas de (DEU), Minister of the Interior, Federal Ministry of the Interior

Makan, Divesh (USA), CEO, ICONIQ Capital

Malcomson, Scott (USA), Author; President, Monere Ltd.

Markwalder, Christa (CHE), President of the National Council and the Federal Assembly

McArdle, Megan (USA), Columnist, Bloomberg View

Michel, Charles (BEL), Prime Minister

Micklethwait, John (USA), Editor-in-Chief, Bloomberg LP

Minton Beddoes, Zanny (GBR), Editor-in-Chief, The Economist

Mitsotakis, Kyriakos (GRC), President, New Democracy Party

Morneau, Bill (CAN), Minister of Finance

Mundie, Craig J. (USA), Principal, Mundie & Associates

Murray, Charles A. (USA), W.H. Brady Scholar, American Enterprise Institute

Netherlands, H.M. the King of the (NLD)

Noonan, Michael (IRL), Minister for Finance

Noonan, Peggy (USA), Author, Columnist, The Wall Street Journal

O'Leary, Michael (IRL), CEO, Ryanair Plc

Ollongren, Kajsa (NLD), Deputy Mayor of Amsterdam

Özel, Soli (TUR), Professor, Kadir Has University

Papalexopoulos, Dimitri (GRC), CEO, Titan Cement Co.

Petraeus, David H. (USA), Chairman, KKR Global Institute

Philippe, Edouard (FRA), Mayor of Le Havre

Pind, Søren (DNK), Minister of Justice

Ratti, Carlo (ITA), Director, MIT Senseable City Lab

Reisman, Heather M. (CAN), Chair and CEO, Indigo Books & Music Inc.

Rubin, Robert E. (USA), Co-Chair, Council on Foreign Relations

Rutte, Mark (NLD), Prime Minister

Sawers, John (GBR), Chairman and Partner, Macro Advisory Partners

Schäuble, Wolfgang (DEU), Minister of Finance

Schieder, Andreas (AUT), Chairman, Social Democratic Group

Schmidt, Eric E. (USA), Executive Chairman, Alphabet Inc.

Scholten, Rudolf (AUT), CEO, Oesterreichische Kontrollbank AG

Schwab, Klaus (INT), Executive Chairman, World Economic Forum

Sikorski, Radoslaw (POL), Senior Fellow, Harvard University; Former Minister of Foreign Affairs

Simsek, Mehmet (TUR), Deputy Prime Minister

Sinn, Hans-Werner (DEU), Professor for Economics and Public Finance, Ludwig Maximilian University of Munich

Skogen Lund, Kristin (NOR), Director General, The Confederation of Norwegian Enterprise

Standing, Guy (GBR), Co-President, BIEN; Research Professor, University of London

Thiel, Peter A. (USA), President, Thiel Capital

Tillich, Stanislaw (DEU), Minister-President of Saxony

Vetterli, Martin (CHE), President, NSF

Wahlroos, Björn (FIN), Chairman, Sampo Group, Nordea Bank, UPM-Kymmene Corporation

Wallenberg, Jacob (SWE), Chairman, Investor AB

Weder di Mauro, Beatrice (CHE), Professor of Economics, University of Mainz

Wolf, Martin H. (GBR), Chief Economics Commentator, Financial Times

The Council on Foreign Relations (CFR) is an offshoot of the Bilderberg Group and consists of well-paid academics and the most influential of politicians. Many of those working in the U.S. entertainment and news industries are on the list of members; they have an agenda and they follow orders. They are told to chip away, bit by bit, our values and morals until we become so desensitized to what we see that nothing surprises us anymore. Through the minds of our young, in school and on TV, the globalist agenda is beginning to seep through the crust.

The CFR, was initially led by J.P. Morgan and later by the Rockefellers, and remains the most powerful political group in America today. The CFR members control both government and "private-industry" news organizations giving them the ability to control what people are seeing. Round Table Groups, formed by individual nations within the CFR, were set up to control the news sources in their countries by controlling the dialog. Through propaganda, the Council on Foreign Relations callously manipulates American Citizens into accepting a certain narrative, one approved by the Round Table Groups that fits into their agenda for the world. The Council on Foreign Relations members all understand the confidentiality they work under but sometimes things get leaked.

The Bilderberg branches extend in all directions. These are but a few of them:

The Royal Institute of International Affairs
Council on Foreign Relations
Canadian Institute of International Affairs
Australian Institute of International Affairs
New Zealand Institute of International Affairs

Danish Institute of International Affairs

Japan Institute of International Affairs

Institute of International Relations, Prague

Institute of International Affairs, Italy

Swedish Institute of International Affairs

Netherlands Institute of International Relations

Norwegian Institute of International Affairs

South African Institute of International Affairs

Institute of International Relations Prague

Austrian Institute for International Affairs

Finnish Institute of International Affairs

Chinese Institute for International Studies

The Real Instituto Elcano de Estudios Internacionales y Estrategicos

The Chicago Council on Foreign Relations

The Psychological Strategy Board a.k.a. The Operations Coordination Board a.k.a. The Special Group. After abolishing the Special Group on February 19, 1961, President John F. Kennedy issued the following statement:

"No President ever wrote or signed an Executive order establishing the Special Group. No President had a way of abolishing the Special Group. The Special Group was not established by

Executive Order, it established itself. This was no accident. This was illegal." When Kennedy killed the Operations Coordination Board, the Special Group continued to operate as if everything was normal, even in the absence of a designated Presidential representative.

"Where did this group and its authority come from? And who funds this group now?" I imagine it is the same as it always has been, the Bilderbergs created it and are funding it, as the special group is alive and well in 2016 and working in cooperation with the following departments:

1. The Secretary of State
2. The Secretary of Defense
3. The Director of The CIA
4. Mossad (Israeli Institute for Intelligence and Special Operations),
5. Israel none of which are elected officials

The CFR continues to control the lives of the people without their knowledge or understanding, through well designed psychological manipulation. The Internet makes their job easier. So many people, myself included, sit behind their keyboards, not venturing beyond it most of the time. We build these virtual worlds around us and these worlds rob us of our present and our future because we live in this one moment. Because of instant access to the world, we never live our real lives because we created a reality based on an imaginary life.

Living in an alternate reality where information is free-flowing, the job of the CFR becomes much easier. Group mentality takes over, and typically, whoever screams the loudest will get heard and their opinion will become fact, just because they said it first and someone repeated it. If you repeat a falsehood long enough, it will become fact eventually. Through psychological manipulation, the CFR can get people to do things even if those things are not in their best interest. The herd mentality will kick in and they will still do it because the group is doing it. This behavior is predictable and necessary for the powers to be able to subdue the people and get them to accept the creation of a one world order under their control.

The Trilateral Commission founded by David Rockefeller controlled Chase Manhattan Bank. Rockefeller first introduced the idea of the Trilateral commission at an annual meeting of the

Bilderberg group held in Knokke, Belgium in the spring of 1972.

The Bilderberg group and the Trilateral Commission are both heavily funded and influenced by the Rockefeller empire, and composed of international financiers, industrialists, media magnates, union bosses, academics and political figures. The purpose of the commission was to engineer a partnership among the ruling powers of North America, Western Europe and Japan, or 'Trilateral', to safeguard, if necessary, the interests of Western capitalism in a volatile world.

David Rockefeller selected all the Trilateral members personally and he funded the commission entirely. David Rockefeller alone decided who was asked to participate and who was not. The commission was totally private and was able to organize without anyone noticing.

David Rockefeller and Prof. Zbigniew Brzezinski of Columbia University, author of the book entitled "Between Two Ages" began the process of selecting from among the "Trilateral" nations the several hundred elite power brokers who would be permitted to join in Trilateral policymaking in the coming years.

One of the commission's primary goals was to place a Trilateral-influenced president in the White House in 1976. Looking for someone they could groom, they chose a few, then settled on an obscure one-term Democratic governor of Georgia, Jimmy Carter, to join the commission.

Carter definitely impressed Rockefeller and Brzezinski, and they viewed Carter as a possible Trilateral candidate. Carter obtained an edge when he opened up trade offices for the state of Georgia in Brussels and Tokyo. That act seemed to fit their concept of the Trilateral mind-set.

Carter was introduced to the other Trilateralists as an ideal presidential candidate by Rockefeller. That meeting took place at the first annual meeting in Kyoto, Japan in May of 1975. Carter announced his bid for the 1976 Democratic presidential nomination, and with Rockefeller's support behind him and his campaign, Carter had the advantage.

Carter campaigned as a "populist" candidate, claiming to be a "man of the people", an "outsider" with no ties to the Establishment, but in fact, Carter was an elitist and an insider; the Trilateral Commission's "hero on a white horse."Rockefeller and Brzezinski helped Carter win the Democratic Presidential nomination.

With the power of the commission, the Rockefeller empire and its media influence behind him, Carter made his way to the presidency, establishing the first full-fledged Trilateral administration, appointing numerous Trilateralists to key policymaking positions and carrying out the Trilateral agenda to the hilt.

In David Rockefeller's book "Memoirs" he admits being a part of a secret clique working to destroy the U.S., then create a new world order. Here is the direct quote from David Rockefeller's book, pg 405:

"Some even believe we [Rockefeller family] are part of a secret cabal working against the best interests of the United States, characterizing my family and me as 'internationalists' and of conspiring with others around the world to build a more integrated global political and economic structure – One World, if you will. If that's the charge, I stand guilty, and I am proud of it."

Rockefeller continued, "We are grateful to The Washington Post, The New York Times, Time Magazine and other great publications whose directors have attended our meetings and respected their promises of discretion for almost forty years. It would have been impossible for us to develop our plan for the world if we had been subject to the bright lights of publicity during those years. But, the work is now much more sophisticated and prepared to march towards a World Government. The supranational sovereignty of an intellectual elite and world bankers is surely preferable to the national auto-determination practiced in past centuries" –David Rockefeller to Trilateral Commission in 1991[27].

Most will find this eye-opening and horrific, but Nick Rockefeller once said, "The end goal is to get everybody chipped, to control the whole society, to have the bankers and the elite people control the world."–Nick Rockefeller during an Aaron Russo interview[28].

I know you want to say to yourself, "No way are these few people, wealthy or not, conspiring against humanity." But they are.

At the 2016 meeting, the Bilderberg Group, will almost certainly be discussing ways to prevent Donald Trump from becoming president even if it means conjuring up some crisis. If they claim there will be mass riots as a result of wealth inequality, the migrant crisis, as well as Brexit; don't believe them.

The Bilderberg 2016 Annual Meeting came and went, and again, the sun still came up the next morning. There were no catastrophes in the night, the moon still shown and a new day greeted us when we woke. We must stop listening to their rhetoric and listen to our hearts.

Hillary Clinton will continue the Muslim onslaught, abolish our Second Amendment and confiscate our guns. She will finish bankrupting our country, so that we can never recover, while other world leaders are doing the same. Our jobs will be gone and the ones left will be taken by illegals or Obama's and Clinton's Arab migrants. Wages will be depressed, resources depleted and crime will ensue. And if you don't believe any of this you have been living in a bubble.

The world leaders have a plan. They plan to let all this happen while they quietly retreat to their rightful utopia. The members of the Bilderbergs, the Council on Foreign Affairs, the Trilateral Commission and others will step up and in a pretense of "saving humanity" they will take dominion over everyone.

We are in a battle for freedom, the freedom of our nation and our citizens. Whereas, Clinton and the rest are determined to be the first to usher in The New World Order, there are still plenty who consider themselves "Nationalists" and plan to stop Globalism and the elites. They come from all walks of life, from all corners of the globe, all backgrounds and varying levels of education; but they all have one thing in common, they have come to an uneasy understanding of what is actually taking place. They have been paying attention and see the signs. The Globalists are leading us down a path of no return but the Nationalists are determined to stop them. The resignation of David Cameron and the Brexit vote were the first steps. There are many more to take.

There is a silent majority even still in 2016 despite the violent threats and intimidation directed at those who support the Nationalist route. But those silent types will be voting on election day and hopefully, like Great Britain, America will be strong enough to stand up and be counted. This is America's last chance and the choice is stark. Do we choose Hillary's Globalism or do we choose Trump's America? This is not the time to be silent any more.

The Declaration of Independence

CONGRESS, July 4, 1776.

The unanimous Declaration of the thirteen united States of America.

"When in the Course of human events, it becomes necessary for one people to dissolve the political bands which have connected them with another, and to assume among the powers of the earth, the separate and equal station to which the Laws of Nature and of Nature's God entitle them, a decent respect to the opinions of mankind requires that they should declare the causes which impel them to the separation.

We hold these truths to be self-evident, that all men are created equal, that they are endowed by their Creator with certain unalienable Rights, that among these are Life, Liberty and the pursuit of Happiness.--That to secure these rights, Governments are instituted among Men, deriving their just powers from the consent of the governed, --That whenever any Form of Government becomes destructive of these ends, it is the Right of the People to alter or to abolish it, and to institute new Government, laying its foundation on such principles and organizing its powers in such form, as to them shall seem most likely to affect their Safety and Happiness. Prudence, indeed, will dictate that Governments long established should not be changed for light and transient causes; and accordingly all experience hath shown, that mankind are more disposed to suffer, while evils are suffer-able, than to right themselves by abolishing the forms to which they are accustomed. But when a long train of abuses and usurpations, pursuing invariably the same Object evinces a design to reduce them under absolute Despotism, it is their right, it is their duty, to throw off such Government, and to provide new Guards for their future security.--Such has been the patient sufferance of these Colonies; and such is now the necessity which constrains them to alter their former Systems of Government. The history of the present King of Great Britain is a history of repeated injuries and usurpations, all having in direct object the establishment of an absolute

Tyranny over these States. To prove this, let Facts be submitted to a candid world.

He has refused his Assent to Laws, the most wholesome and necessary for the public good.

He has forbidden his Governors to pass Laws of immediate and pressing importance, unless suspended in their operation till his Assent should be obtained; and when so suspended, he has utterly neglected to attend to them.

He has refused to pass other Laws for the accommodation of large districts of people, unless those people would relinquish the right of Representation in the Legislature, a right inestimable to them and formidable to tyrants only.

He has called together legislative bodies at places unusual, uncomfortable, and distant from the depository of their public Records, for the sole purpose of fatiguing them into compliance with his measures.

He has dissolved Representative Houses repeatedly, for opposing with manly firmness his invasions on the rights of the people.

He has refused for a long time, after such dissolutions, to cause others to be elected; whereby the Legislative powers, incapable of Annihilation, have returned to the People at large for their exercise; the State remaining in the mean time exposed to all the dangers of invasion from without, and convulsions within.

He has endeavored to prevent the population of these States; for that purpose obstructing the Laws for Naturalization of Foreigners; refusing to pass others to encourage their migrations hither, and raising the conditions of new Appropriations of Lands.

He has obstructed the Administration of Justice, by refusing his Assent to Laws for establishing Judiciary powers.

He has made Judges dependent on his Will alone, for the tenure of their offices, and the amount and payment of their salaries.

He has erected a multitude of New Offices, and sent hither swarms of Officers to harass our people, and eat out their substance.

He has kept among us, in times of peace, Standing Armies without the Consent of our legislatures.

He has affected to render the Military independent of and superior to the Civil power.

He has combined with others to subject us to a jurisdiction foreign to our constitution, and unacknowledged by our laws; giving his Assent to their Acts of pretended Legislation:

For Quartering large bodies of armed troops among us:

For protecting them, by a mock Trial, from punishment for any Murders which they should commit on the Inhabitants of these States:

For cutting off our Trade with all parts of the world:

For imposing Taxes on us without our Consent:

For depriving us in many cases, of the benefits of Trial by Jury:

For transporting us beyond Seas to be tried for pretended offenses

For abolishing the free System of English Laws in a neighboring Province, establishing therein an Arbitrary government, and enlarging its Boundaries so as to render it at once an example and fit instrument for introducing the same absolute rule into these Colonies:

For taking away our Charters, abolishing our most valuable Laws, and altering fundamentally the Forms of our Governments:

For suspending our own Legislatures, and declaring themselves invested with power to legislate for us in all cases whatsoever.

He has abdicated Government here, by declaring us out of his Protection and waging War against us.

He has plundered our seas, ravaged our Coasts, burnt our towns, and destroyed the lives of our people.

He is at this time transporting large Armies of foreign Mercenaries to complete the works of death, desolation and tyranny, already begun with circumstances of Cruelty & perfidy scarcely paralleled in the most barbarous ages, and totally unworthy the Head of a civilized nation.

He has constrained our fellow Citizens taken Captive on the high Seas to bear Arms against their Country, to become the executioners of their friends and Brethren, or to fall themselves by their Hands.

He has excited domestic insurrections amongst us, and has endeavored to bring on the inhabitants of our frontiers, the merciless Indian Savages, whose known rule of warfare, is an undistinguished destruction of all ages, sexes and conditions.

In every stage of these Oppressions We have Petitioned for Redress in the most humble terms: Our repeated Petitions have been answered only by repeated injury. A Prince whose character is thus marked by every act which may define a Tyrant, is unfit to be the ruler of a free people.

Nor have We been wanting in attentions to our British brethren. We have warned them from time to time of attempts by their legislature to extend an unwarrantable jurisdiction over us. We have reminded them of the circumstances of our emigration and settlement here. We have appealed to their native justice and magnanimity, and we have conjured them by the ties of our common kindred to disavow these usurpations, which, would inevitably interrupt our connections and correspondence. They too have been deaf to the voice of justice and of consanguinity. We must, therefore, acquiesce in the necessity, which denounces our Separation, and hold them, as we hold the rest of mankind, Enemies in War, in Peace Friends.

We, therefore, the Representatives of the united States of America, in General Congress,

Assembled, appealing to the Supreme Judge of the world for the rectitude of our intentions, do, in the Name, and by Authority of the good People of these Colonies, solemnly publish and declare, That these United Colonies are, and of Right ought to be Free and Independent States; that they are Absolved from all Allegiance to the British Crown, and that all political connection between them and the State of Great Britain, is and ought to be totally dissolved; and that as Free and Independent States, they have full Power to levy War, conclude Peace, contract Alliances, establish Commerce, and to do all other Acts and Things which Independent States may of right do. And for the support of this Declaration, with a firm reliance on the protection of divine Providence, we mutually pledge to each other our Lives, our Fortunes and our sacred Honor."

PART 2

AMERICA FIRST

DONALD TRUMP

"This wave of globalization has wiped out totally, TOTALLY our middle class."

Donald Trump."

PART 2

INTRODUCTION

The pundits, commentators, and politicians will all try to explain away this movement that is Donald Trump. This wasn't supposed to happen, but here we are. Donald Trump has brought out voters like no candidate before him. He is drawing all demographics; from women, like me, Hispanics, Evangelicals, African-Americans, Whites, Muslims, working class Americans with no college degree; the college educated, the LGBT community, the elderly, the Vets, the Millennial with college debt, and on and on. Donald Trump's appeal seems to cross all lines and genders and the "experts" can't explain it.

A Trump supporter, on the other hand, can explain it. They come from all walks of life but the one thing they all have in common is their love for America. They are patriots who work hard and the future of our country, for our next generation, is of the utmost importance to them.

A Trump supporter of my generation doesn't care about himself, instead thinking only about the future. Most can't even begin to fathom a Hillary Clinton presidency, much less imagine what the world will become under her administration.

This election season started off with immigration being the important issue for most, but in the past two or three months, another issue has reared its ugly head.

Hillary Clinton and Barack Obama have admitted to being globalists who aspire to the idealistic globalist agenda. It is this revelation that is waking up America and driving patriotic Americans into action. This idea of a New World Order with a handful of rich people making all the decisions has sent shock waves through the people. They understand now what this election is really all about. It is about Globalism vs. Nationalism: Clinton vs. Trump.

Globalists began their subtle yet consistent capturing of society a long time when they got a majority of the country's media and elite universities to sign on to their agenda. Next they directed their attention to Hollywood, think tanks, charitable foundations, corporations, and banks.

Decades ago and innocently enough, they began teaching our children about diversity, inclusion and the global agenda. Today's Millennial is more accepting of almost anything because they were taught globalism over nationalism. Without the majority even realizing it, we have been force fed globalism for years.

The elites thought they had it all sewn up and that their plan was going according to schedule. Hillary Clinton was supposed to waltz into the election of 2016 and walk away coronated.

The arrogance of the politicians and the media this past year has gone way beyond anything ever before. That fact alone has made people angry and forced them to open their eyes and pay attention. The people realize now whose side their government is on and they are madder than hornets because they know the government doesn't care. The globalist government sees their agenda within reach and they will not let some pesky citizen take that away from them. As far as the government is concerned, you mean nothing to them.

Then along comes Donald Trump who crashes their party with a bang. Nobody saw it coming, especially Hillary Clinton. Donald Trump has upset the apple cart and Hillary experienced déjà vu when Barack Obama came out of nowhere and stole the coronation from her, too.

Americans hate the thought of globalism; most of them anyway, and they will tolerate almost anything except having their sovereignty and freedoms ripped away by liberals with an agenda.

Most every dagger that Donald Trump has thrown at the Democrats happens to be anti-globalist and pro-nationalist. This definite signal of nationalism to the people is what is driving his rapidly historic rise.

As a Nationalist, Donald Trump believes that any real nation must have clearly defined and secure borders, otherwise it isn't really a nation. Like patriots everywhere, Trump also believes that our history, culture and heritage are sacred and should be protected, therefore immigration must be controlled. Uncontrolled mass immigration from anywhere undermines who we are as a people and destroys the heritage of a nationalistic nation.

Globalists detest borders and they won't stop until we are a borderless world, well aside from the borders that enclose their own personal homes and workplace, that is. They believe that sovereignty is obsolete, over-rated and has no place in their

Globalist utopia. They prefer a totally inter-connected world with information, money, goods and people speeding around the globe without regard to the traditional limits of distance and borders.

Globalists are typically humanitarians with an "I will save the world," mentality. The globalist believes that the rights and well-being of the world's people supersede the rights and well-being of America or any other nation.

Globalists, in an effort to advance foreign policy, are quick to foment events around the world to create an atmosphere that justifies their call for a global world. Even with all this supposed "humanitarianism" the globalist really doesn't care about the world, environment or the people in it. It is all about dominating world events in order to dominate the world.

Nationalists want their country to be safe with a powerful military, respect throughout the world; and most importantly, they want America's wellbeing to come first. The struggles of people around the globe, however heartbreaking they may be, doesn't fit within nationalist considerations. We help where we can but the fate of America is always the priority.

Trade in America has been on all sides of the spectrum depending on who was in charge. It has gone from nationalist to protectionist to most recently, the globalist attempt as we may just see a globalist world within our lifetime if we elect Hillary Clinton.

Globalists encourage the free flow of goods across non-existent borders on the theory that this trade will benefit all nations and will eventually lead to a global economy.

Whether they are right or not, the nationalist focus is solely on the American citizen whose lives and livelihoods have been dramatically altered by the anemic recovery of the Barack Obama recession years. The day-to-day suffering of everyday Americans is what has driven this powerful new interest in protectionism. Every day, ordinary patriots are making themselves heard with a resounding, "Enough," and Globalist elites are running for cover, trying hard not to be seen.

Political Correctness is a cancer on our society. Elite institutions, universities and other liberal academia have used their positions of power to determine the conversation. They have taken political correctness to a ridiculous level, telling people what to say and how to feel, who to accept and who to support and if you don't follow their rules, they will destroy you professionally and personally. They hate Middle America and love to ridicule ordinary citizens then stifle any feedback through intimidation and demagoguery.

The rise of Donald Trump shows us just how angry the electorate really is. Trump's "no time for political correctness" attitude has struck a chord with the people and for the first time in a long time people feel like they have a voice.

The words racist, homophobe, islamophobe, and xenophobe are beginning to mean nothing to the average person. They have been called these things for so long that the words have lost their meaning for most people. The 2016 Nationalist says, "Call us whatever you want. Stick and stones."

They send their kids to college with hopes of a better future, instead the college kid is hit with political correctness and all the dos and don'ts. If they are a Conservative individual, they learn fast they their ideas and views aren't allowed on campus but instead are banned as inappropriate and intolerable for other college kids to hear.

People are saying, "No more political correctness. If you can't take the heat, get out of the kitchen."

Pride in one's nation is an inherent trait found in the nationalist. They care about their history, ancestors, and heritage and they pass this knowledge and wisdom down through the generations to be used; as much as to be preserved. Globalists don't have that kind of pride and they don't hesitate to assault the nationalists for it.

As so much of our history is being re-written by liberal democrats, our children are not learning the true history of our nation and what makes America so great. This omission of pride and exceptionalism in our schools history books was an intentional and integral part of getting them used to globalism. Nationalists feel that everything America stands for is under assault with this election and the globalists are the ones leading that assault.

Donald Trump supporters are tired of the power of the influential class controlling and changing this great country. They were yearning for a voice, for someone to hear them. Congress and the states weren't listening either and even though some of the people were screaming to be heard, only one man heard their cries.

Donald Trump heard them loud and clear and he became their messenger. He not only attacked illegal immigration but did it sincerely without pandering and looked people straight in the eyes and said he would put a stop to it.

In spite of some of his more cringe-worthy statements like "I could stand in the middle of 5th Avenue and shoot somebody and I wouldn't lose voters," or perhaps because of it, patriotic Americans began to listen and today they flock to his rallies in droves.

Donald Trump personifies "America First" when he questions foreign policy decisions like continuing with NAFTA and NATO. He poses the questions when nobody else is willing; just asking the questions sets the elites on edge. As it turns out many Americans are asking the same questions and they like Donald Trump answers.

Trump says he will solve our trade problems, fix our immigration and build a wall, bring back jobs and give Americans hope again and he will do all this without taking a dime of tax-payer money as salary. Without being politically correct, Trump unequivocally states that as

President, he will consider America first and foremost in every decision he makes. He promises to never stop fighting for the people of America and he will not rest until he has restored America as America was supposed to be. And Donald Trump says, "We're going to be saying Merry Christmas again, folks."

Hillary Clinton, meanwhile, is the personification of the globalist elite: open borders, humanitarian interventionist, a free trader, totally in sync with political correctness; a practitioner of identity politics. She will play any and all cards (race, gender, etc.) she has in order to get what she wants.

It's impossible to say at this early stage in the political season whether Trump, the 2016 Americanism candidate actually has a chance to win the U.S. Presidency; but win or lose, he has turned the political system upside down with powerful new rhetoric on his stance on nationalism and globalism. Donald Trump isn't going away anytime soon. For the globalist elites of America, it's an entirely new ball-game.

"Whatever America
hopes to bring to pass
in the world must first
come to pass in the
heart of America."

Dwight D. Eisenhower

CHAPTER 12

AMERICA FIRST

Donald Trump has energy like I have never seen before. He is a non-stop powerhouse who never quits and seldom loses. He is one of those rare people that once you meet him, you are never the same again. He exudes confidence. Trump has a calming effect on people because there is a sincerity that you can see and feel. You know that when he tells you something, he is telling the truth, like it or not.

Trump has managed to keep my vote through this past year and a half. I won't lie, there have been plenty of times when he opened his mouth and what came out made me cringe. He is brash, bold, loudmouthed; certainly not politically correct and sometimes he crosses the line. But I don't think Americans care all that much about his rough exterior because the words he is saying is what they have been longing to hear. Donald Trump's policies fall right in line with what the American people, want but until now, have not been allowed to voice. Political correctness has silenced anything good and allowed for a moral-less mind-set accepting of all things once considered taboo.

Donald Trump has been brave enough to come forward and say the hard words. He is determined and his methods are effective. He is an internationally respected and adored businessman who knows how to get things done. If America needs change, Donald Trump is the one to actually deliver it.

He is an outsider; a businessman turned politician whom no one, myself included, ever thought would get this far. Most of us suspected that the media or one of the other 16 candidates would get the best of him and he would be gone. Some thought he would just get bored and bail on his supporters, leaving us alongside the road as he dashed back to his rich and fabulous life. None of that happened and since securing the 2016 GOP Presidential Nomination at the Cleveland Convention, he has been rejuvenated. He is elated and it shows in his rallies. They are energetic and with only the occasional use of a teleprompter, Donald Trump woos the crowd - and they adore him.

Donald Trump is a breath of fresh air for a nation that is suffocating. Like some of us, he has grandchildren too, and he wants them to be proud of their country and to know what and who America really is; where we came from and what we have overcome. Most of all, I think he wants them to be proud of their grandpa. Donald Trump is just like any parent or grandparent. He wants to be able to look his grandchildren in the eye and tell them how hard we fought for them; that we never gave up and we won the war. America is now, and forevermore, will be the land of the free, home to families full of pride and hope. America is still a place where everyone has a chance to make a difference. That is the country we grew up in and we want that to be the America our grandchildren and great grand-children know and love.

Donald Trump has made no secret of his America First, anti-Globalist positions and addresses it most days nonetheless through his comments on Trade.

Trump has openly criticized the Trans-Pacific Partnership (TPP trade deal), and Hillary Clinton's history of support. The deal is awaiting ratification in Congress and if Trump has his way, it will never be ratified. Clinton claims there is nothing wrong with the deal but Donald Trump describes it as "the deathblow for American manufacturing jobs."

Trump has promised to renegotiate the North American Free Trade Agreement (NAFTA) to get a more equitable deal for American workers. Trump also threatened to withdraw from the deal altogether and start over if his proposals aren't agreed upon. The North American Free Trade Agreement was signed by Bill Clinton and has proven to be a disaster for our nation's job market, costing us almost five million manufacturing jobs from 1997 to 2014 alone. The TPP would be the final nail in the coffin for American economics.

Donald Trump has vowed to bring back U.S. manufacturing jobs by creating incentives for companies to move their jobs back to the U.S. This will help our disastrous unemployment numbers, but also the revenue stream and will stimulate the economy. Trump has also mentioned slapping tariffs on goods produced by (American) companies that move manufacturing jobs offshore. Some like that idea; some do not. But whichever way you fall on an issue, we know that trade deals must work for all parties involved.

Trump didn't leave much room for doubt on his anti-Globalist stance. In his famous "America First Speech," he made it clear his only interest right now was America and her problems. After we put our own house in order, we can then tackle a few of the world's problems. But security begins at home and we must be a united and protected America. We must fight for something we believe in now because the future is depending on us.

Trump will build up our military and take care of our Vets. He will repeal and replace Obamacare which is expected to implode in 2017 anyway. He has promised to get premiums down to something we can all afford and will encourage competition, letting the free-market have a say in medical costs for once.

He has promised to build a wall on our southern border. This is a controversial issue, but one that is on the top of everyone's list of primary concerns this election season, whether they admit it or not.

Immigration into the U.S. is becoming intolerable as truckloads of unvetted Syrian migrants and illegals are dumped into small cities in the middle of the night. Often the numbers of imports exceed the actual population of the small town; overwhelming the citizens. Some of these people have proven to have sinister intentions and have committed violent crimes while here, but that doesn't stop our government from taking them in anyway and dispersing them through our neighborhoods, without any regard for anyone's safety.

Donald Trump has traveled the world and he didn't have to step into this political arena; he could have stayed at home to enjoy his life of wealth and comfort and who would blame him?

Donald Trump, however, wouldn't be able to live with himself if he didn't at least give it his best shot. He knows the real path our nation is on and he knows that this is the last chance for America. By his own admission, he watched for decades as stupid politicians made stupid choices. When he saw that America was going over the cliff again, possibly for good this time, Donald Trump decided he had no choice but to step up and give Americans a real leader. The entire Trump family is putting it all on the line to work as hard for our country as they have for the family empire. They are fighting for all of us; the little people who have no voice.

When Donald Trump suggested halting immigration, critics took that to mean all Muslim immigration, but in fact, he was speaking about "illegal" immigration. He never said he wanted to send people back who came here legally, and that is where the media likes to distort events. Trump did indicate that if a crime was involved, then a deportation may follow but I am sure we can all agree that in today's climate, we have to be extra careful whom we let in our borders. This is not the time for open borders when there are so many dangerous people in the world.

Donald Trump understands the dangers and he knows how to fight them. He wants to secure our borders and make us safe again. He will create jobs for the American Citizens who call this country "home." Whether you see him "live" at a rally or watch on one of the many Internet sites that stream his rallies, you feel a connection to him. He consistently says the same things, hammering our current government, Hillary Clinton's corruption and lies, and the never-ending immigrant influx, which Trump declares, "Could very well be the great Trojan Horse of our time."

And Donald Trump may well be right. I am sure there are places in Europe right now that feel like they have been blindsided by the sheer number of migrants and the crimes that follow them. I imagine the people who live in the worst affected parts of Europe wish they could go back and stop the migration before it got out of hand. America still has that chance. We can vote for America's sovereignty and we can follow Brexit and say no to mass immigration and globalism. We can repair our own torn society and rebuild; having pride in our accomplishments and confidence in ourselves.

Donald Trump wants us to be proud to be Americans again with a never-quit attitude and pride in being a nationalist. When America has reestablished her strength in the world, we can begin to rebuild our nation, our communities and our individual lives.

Older generations have yearned to hear this "America First" rhetoric from a Presidential candidate but a lot of Millennials wanted absolutely nothing to do with Donald Trump.

To them, he's a fast-talking know-it-all, a hustler, a BS'er of the first order; an egotist, a narcissist, and an avid racist, especially after he used the word "nationalist".

The Millennials have been conditioned to think that the word "nationalist" is a dirty word and that their pride should come from their globalist upbringing. Whereas some are taken in by this belief, some are seeing the real truths play out in their own lives. They are deep in debt coming out of college with no job and little prospects. They see redistribution of wealth taking place, just not in their direction.

Our college kids are recognizing that our government makes more money off them through student loan debt interest than any other program they run. In my opinion and in the opinion of most of the country, the student loan program is the one program where our government should really not make a dime. Our kids should be allowed to go to college and come out with manageable debt. Our government gives loans to corporations with little to no interest, yet they are making boatloads of money off the backs of our next generation of wage earners. As our kids start out their lives crushed with college debt, it is becoming unsustainable as jobs and benefits are going to the migrants and illegals first. This is beginning to open the eyes of the Millennial, but although some still look at Donald Trump with apprehension, they are willing to listen to what he has to say.

My generation, the parents of the millennials, are not ready to see the country we all grew up in turned over to a globalist regime. Too many people died to make America what it is and my generation wants to honor them by keeping America free and a land of prosperity.

Donald Trump supporters have been called ignorant, low-information, low-rent people who are racist and bigots and are just caught up in Trump's rock-star like persona and are not listening to his inflammatory words; but they would assure you, they are listening.

I still watch the Trump rallies and they keep getting bigger. I have been to four of them with my Uncle Larry, getting there eight hours ahead of time to be first in line. I hear now that the lines begin to form about twelve hours ahead of opening. If you plan to go and want to shake his hand, I suggest you get there early!!

I see crowds of ten, twelve and even fourteen thousand, with over-flow rooms bulging and still more trying to get in the doors.

Donald Trump has done something I have never seen done before and the American people are loving it. They love it so much that everyday his support grows as Trump effortlessly flushes out the rats who have been burrowing deep within our political world and the media.

One by one Donald Trump has forced them out into the light and when they show themselves, the American people are waiting with a trap. We are ready to clean up our government and the media, end the corruption and the Clinton's pay-for-play regime. America cannot survive a President Clinton; and Globalism will benefit no one except for those who are already rich and powerful. The middle class is forgotten under globalism.

Donald Trump wants to stop globalism before it becomes the norm and restore us to the people we were before; full of hope, full of pride, ready to take on the big issues and win. Donald Trump doesn't see Americans as ordinary, as he told a young woman at a rally once; "You are not ordinary, you are special, first" and he believes this about everyone.

Donald trust believes in Americanism and he is asking for everyone to stand with him and with pride in their hearts, vote on November 8th, 2016.

Hillary Clinton's former opponent, Bernie Sanders, agrees with Donald Trump on globalism and the unfair trade imbalances.

In an editorial for the New York Times, Sanders wrote the following excerpt with regards to globalism and trade:

"In the last 15 years, nearly 60,000 factories in this country have closed, and more than 4.8 million well-paid manufacturing jobs have disappeared. Much of this is related to disastrous (Globalist) trade agreements that encourage corporations to move to low-wage countries..." Sanders continued.

"We need to fundamentally reject our 'free trade' policies and move to fair trade. Americans should not have to compete against workers in low-wage countries who earn pennies an hour. We must defeat the Trans-Pacific Partnership (TPP)."

As expected, Bernie points out that this endeavor should be led by "a new Democratic President," and though he doesn't say Hillary Clinton by name, he does denounce Donald Trump.

Sanders seemed to understand globalism too, and the negative effects it will have on the world, but in the end, Bernie Sanders folded to the

Clinton machine, even going so far as endorsing her, which understandably infuriated Bernie Sanders supporters.

Most voters felt bad for Sanders, regardless of party, because we all watched as Hillary stole the primary from him. Her ability to garner Super-delegates gave her a tremendous advantage over Sanders. With a completely rigged-for-her primary using Debbie Wasserman Schultz and the DNC, poor Sanders didn't stand a chance. Even in states he won, Clinton received the majority of the delegates. We all smelled a rat, but what were we to do? This was Bernie's battle to fight and he chose not to fight it.

Americans on the other hand took notice of the dirty, deceitful and completely rigged system, which always ran in favor of the establishment and the status quo instead of the voters. Trump has done us all a favor and torn away the curtain to expose the ugliness that is globalism.

The globalist are not happy with Donald Trump's plans to shut down their personal money machines by canceling NAFTA and refusing to ratify the TPP as these are essential components of the Globalist agenda. Instead, Trump is talking about using tariffs to punish U.S. companies who ship manufacturing jobs overseas. He is talking about getting rid of 3/4's of the regulations strangling small business and allow them to grow and create jobs. Donald Trump is a negotiator and a builder. He understands better than anyone how to get things done and he doesn't like the globalists and their agenda anymore than they like him.

There are tremendous forces against Trump winning this election but if anyone can pull this off, it is Donald J. Trump. He has the stamina and experience to tackle his enemies head on and he is not afraid of them at all. He stands tall and proud and challenges the status quo, and for that, he has the approval of the American people. We are tired of watching the crooks of the world take advantage of our laws, manipulating them to suit their corrupt ways. Our government is complicate in this fraud as they silence Americans and we are forced to watch our country fall to the enemy within.

Trump makes a clear distinction between Globalism and what's good for America, proving that he understands how those two concepts are completely incompatible with each other. Globalism and Nationalism cannot co-exist or we will see nothing but never-ending battles.

With U.S. factories continuing to close and even more jobs lost, anyone with a brain can see that the American worker is a relic of the past, rarely seen anymore, like the elusive Big Foot.

So where does this leave the voter? On one side we have Hillary Clinton. She's in the pocket of Wall Street, her donors, big Pharma, and she's dedicated to the advancement of Globalism on every possible front (remember her words "it takes a village to raise a child").

She is a known pathological liar who has ties to almost every criminal political scandal for the past three decades. She is the ultimate insider. Her husband, former President Bill Clinton, makes huge amounts of money giving speeches in exchange for favors from the Hillary Clinton State Department. He also attends Bilderberg meetings.

On the other side, we have Donald Trump, who's saying all the right things about immigration, crime in our streets, globalism's impact on America. He seems to be reading the tea leaves, but he just didn't happen on this rhetoric by accident. He is highly intelligent with foresight and an understanding of consequences. He sees things happening based on patterns and behavior, and that is a trait every president should have.

Trump is saying what America would like to say but some people still have reservations because of his hard line and his use of the word Nationalism? He would ask you to listen carefully to his proposals, hear him out, maybe attend a rally or put a banner in your yard. Do something to give yourself hope and keep you focused on the issues at hand.

Trump is telling his supporters to stay strong, don't listen to the dishonest and lying media. Use the Internet to get his message out and never stop moving forward, one day at a time, making change happen.

Globalists want everyone to pledge allegiance to Humanity, the Global Family and the Global Future. It makes them feel superior to say "We're for humanity, we're for everybody else."

So many Americans are out of work and our government is more concerned with the needs of illegals and migrants then they are about our own.

They are openly taking money from the taxpayer and spreading it around to as many corrupt organizations as they can find.

This election and the subsequent Presidency is certainly about the character of the person but it is also much more. Hillary Clinton has proven she is a consistent liar but worse, she is a liar with no remorse. She doesn't care about what happens to this country or to any of us. She cares only about herself and the globalist world that the rich and powerful are building right now. She wants only to take her place in history and have it be told that Hillary Clinton was there at the beginning; she saw it through and she completed her mission. That mission, unfortunately, is our demise.

Donald Trump has a proven record of wanting to protect America and the economy. He wants to make America a safe place to raise our children and he wants everyone to have the opportunities he and his family have had. Donald Trump was motivated into action by the inaction of Barack Obama and Hillary Clinton. With every terrible decision they made, Donald Trump saw a weakening of our country and being the businessman he is, he couldn't sit idly by and watch this happen. If possible, Donald Trump is going to take some action.

"Nations whose nationalism is destroyed are subject to ruin."

Muammar al-Gaddafi

CHAPTER 13

WHAT IS NATIONALISM?

Nationalism is when a group of people feel more significance by being a part of a geographical region, one that seeks independence for every culture of people within the region. This ideology requires the individual to identify with a nation over an individual or global entity.

Pride in country is expressed through national flags, parades, fireworks, beautiful anthems, great food and comfort through togetherness and the camaraderie of fellow patriots.

Throughout history, people have seen the importance of being a part of a group for safety and they began to identify with their country, rather than their smaller town or province. They began to see the benefits of nationalism and they began to develop patriotism.

Patriotic nationalism began to show itself and was being actively promoted by the British government in the mid-18th century for the sake of safety. This was repeated all over the globe in Prussia, Italy, Asia Minor and other areas as the people saw the need for protection. National symbols, anthems, flags and narratives were quickly constructed and adopted so that the nationalist country could be easily identified.

Nationalism vs. Globalism has become one of the most significant political and social discussions of our time. As we have learned, they have both been around for hundreds of years but now is the time of choice as the concepts of globalism are spread quickly using any means possible.

Nationalism exist because of two distinct groups:

1) The Modernist: those who believe that nationalism is a recent phenomenon that requires the structural conditions of modern society in order to exist.

2) The Primordialist: those who believe nationalism is a reflection of the ancient evolutionary tendency of humans to organize into distinct groupings based on an affinity of birth, "like follows like".

Nationalism is an awareness of the importance of humans within the group. The nation is only as strong as its weakest link, so a successful nationalist society must adhere to some rules too.

You are expected to be ready to respond to a group-wide crisis using competition as training. Being able to organize into groups quickly and efficiently assures the success of the group, making defense against hostile groups or conflicts easier to manage and deflect.

Nationalists find that individuals can gain advantages through cooperation with others; in not only securing goods but also in manual labor. They have found that sometimes the group works better than the individual. So why is this different from Globalism?

Control. Globalists want authoritarian control over the remaining population, while Nationalists want only control over their own nation. They want everyone to live free within the nation, and they want personal responsibility for the individual. They believe those are the things needed for a peaceful and free society.

The Primordialist perspective of Nationalism is based upon the Theory of Evolution as it perceives nationalism to be the result of the evolution of human beings into identifying groups, such as ethnic groups, thus forming the foundation of a nation. These groups then recognize smaller group attachments thought to be unique with emotional ties. These are based upon kinship and promoted along lines of common ancestry. They bond with the familiar and this bonding creates Nationalism.

The modernist interpretation of Nationalism perceives that nationalism flourishes in modern societies large enough to have an industrial economy capable of sustaining the society. They must also have a central supreme authority capable of maintaining authority and unity, and a centralized language or small group of centralized languages understood by a community of people. Modernists note that this is only possible in modern societies because traditional societies typically fall short of the requirements.

The question remains, "Which road to take?"

Critics of nationalism have argued that it is often unclear what constitutes a "nation", and why should a nation be the only legitimate unit of political rule.

In 2016, a nation is represented when you look at America. We are a nation and are going to remain a nation if the patriots of this country will stand together. Divided as a nation, we are useless, but together, as a united America, we are formidable. We have been the strength of the world in the past and we will be again.

Nationalism should not be confused with patriotism.

As we know, nationalism is the feeling that one's geographic region is more important than one's self; whereas, patriotism is crucial because pride in one's nation, and a willingness to defend it if necessary, are the basis of national security and independence. Patriotism is the courage that comes from nationalism and the need for self-preservation.

Nationalism and patriotism go hand in hand because if one is lacking then the will to follow is diminished. Nationalism is the idea that one's country is superior to somebody else's. Patriotism is the understanding that your nation is quite exceptional and should be valued and protected.

If we don't have both patriotism and nationalism at this point in 2016, then the world will head to globalism and that path is one-way only.

We can't allow complacency or fear stop us from doing everything we can to stop Hillary Clinton and George Soros. We have to stop the globalist or we become the globalist.

"Battles are won by slaughter and maneuver. The greater the general, the more he contributes in maneuver, the less he demands in slaughter."

Winston Churchill

CHAPTER 14

TRUMP HITS HILLARY

Wednesday, June 22, 2016, the nation watched as Donald Trump steps up his attacks on Hillary Clinton in a speech delivered to the nation at Trump SoHo in New York City.

With our beautiful American flags displayed proudly behind him, Trump speaks openly and honestly about the devastation Clinton has brought down on our country. He has dubbed her "Crooked Hillary" and it is a title that she deservedly has earned.

Donald Trump begins by answering a question he is asked most often, "Why are you running for President?" He stated unequivocally that he is running for one reason only and that is, "To give back to a country that has been so good to me."

He describes a system that is stacked against the American Citizen by stating that the entire economy, as well as the political system, is designed to benefit the elites and not Middle Class America.

"It's rigged by big donors who want to keep down wages. It's rigged by big businesses who want to leave our country, fire our workers, and sell their products back into the U.S. with absolutely no consequences for them. It's rigged by bureaucrats who are trapping kids in failing schools. It's rigged against you, the American people." Trump then implores Bernie Sander's supporters to join his campaign so "We can fix the system" together, "For All Americans." This includes fixing the disastrous trade deals implemented by corrupt, power hungry politicians.

Trump calls Hillary Clinton a "world class liar," as he attacks her "phony landing in Bosnia under fire," claiming she had to run for her life on the tarmac as sniper fired rained down on her. The truth is none of that happened. Clinton was met peacefully by a group of young girls bearing gifts of smiles and flowers. Trump then reminds us that Brian Williams' career was destroyed for lying in much the same manner.

Trump is a Nationalist who believes in Americanism. He is not an Isolationist but wants to end the unfairness and put the American worker first. "We're going to put America First, and we're going to make America great again," Trump says.

Trump says this election will decide whether our nation is ruled by the people or the politicians and Trump promises to end the special interest monopoly that has taken hold of our politicians in Washington D.C.

Trump says Clinton has "perfected the politics of personal profit and even theft." He says Clinton ran the State Department like a "personal hedge fund" while doing favors for oppressive regimes in exchange for tremendous amounts of cash as Secretary of State.

When Clinton left that post, she made $21.6 million giving speeches to Wall Street banks and other special interests in less than 2 years. These are speeches she wants to keep secret, not revealing content to the public. It begs the question, "What does she have to hide?"

Together, Hillary and Bill made $153 million since 2001 by giving speeches to lobbyists, CEOs, and foreign governments. That kind of money doesn't come without strings.

"They totally own her," Trump said about foreign nations' bought and paid for influence over Hillary Clinton, "And that will never change."

The choice in this election is a choice between "taking our government back from the special interests, or surrendering our last scrap of independence to their total and complete control," Trump stated.

Hillary Clinton still thinks that she is entitled to the Presidency, just as she did when she ran against Barack Obama in 2008.

Hillary Clinton's campaign slogan is "I'm with her." But Donald Trump annihilates her slogan with one of his own, "You know what my response to that is?" Trump states, "I'm with you: the American people."

Hillary Clinton believes everything should be all about her and her allegiance is only to herself. Donald Trump's loyalty, on the other hand, is placed squarely with Americans, "I know it's all about you – I know it's all about Making America Great Again for All Americans - FOR ALL AMERICANS."

"Our country lost its way when we stopped putting the American people first," Trump said. "We got here because we switched from a policy of Americanism – focusing on what's good for America's middle class – to a policy of globalism, focusing on how to make money for large corporations who can move their wealth and workers to foreign countries all to the detriment of the American worker and the American economy."

"This is not a rising tide that lifts all boats," he said. "This is a wave of globalization that wipes out our middle class and our jobs."

"We need to reform our economic system so that, once again, we can all succeed together, and America can become rich again. That's what we mean by America First," Trump said to roaring applause.

As you travel across America it becomes obvious what has happened to our nation with the Clinton's and Obama's rapidly growing globalist agenda. In town after town, you see devastation as companies move their factories offshore. People can't find jobs and the jobs that are available are going to illegals and immigrants brought in by the Obama Administration's anti-American immigration and trade policies.

Hillary Clinton is an avid supporter of those policies and will continue them if elected. She supported not only Bill Clinton's disastrous NAFTA, but also China's entrance into the World Trade Organization. Since the signing of those two agreements, our country has lost nearly one-third of its manufacturing jobs.

"Our trade deficit with China soared 40% during Hillary Clinton's time as Secretary of State -- a disgraceful performance for which she should not be congratulated, but rather scorned," Trump says. Clinton also allowed China to steal hundreds of billions of dollars in our intellectual property, a crime which continues to this day.

Hillary Clinton handed China millions of America's best jobs, bankrupting families all across the nation and in return, Hillary Clinton got rich!

Hillary Clinton banks millions of dollars from anti-gay and anti-woman regimes and she wants to infiltrate our country with like-minded migrants from countries she takes money from.

"I only want to admit people who share our values and love our people, (but) Hillary Clinton wants to bring in people who believe women should be enslaved and gays put to death," Trump states. "Maybe her motivation lies among the more than 1,000 foreign donations Hillary failed to disclose while at the State Department." Reportedly, tremendous amounts of money were funneled to Clinton and the Clinton Foundation in one form or another.

"Hillary Clinton accepted $58,000 in jewelry from the government of Brunei when she was Secretary of State – plus millions more for her foundation. The Sultan of Brunei has pushed oppressive Sharia law, including the punishment of death by stoning for being gay," Donald Trump informed the nation.

Trump continues to detail the staggering financial gain Clinton has received through her political career and tenure in the State Department and the favors she passed out to foreign countries. "The government of Brunei also stands to be one of the biggest beneficiaries of Hillary's Trans-Pacific Partnership, which she would absolutely approve if given the chance," Trump added. "Hillary Clinton took up to $25 million from Saudi Arabia, where being gay is also punishable by death." He also pointed out that Clinton "took millions from Kuwait, Qatar, Oman and many other countries that horribly abuse women and LGBT citizens." Those numbers are a mere drop in the bucket when it comes to the payoffs that Hillary Clinton has enjoyed.

In the book "Clinton Cash," Peter Schweitzer brilliantly documents how Bill and Hillary used the State Department to enrich their family at America's expense. Trump states succinctly that, "She gets rich making you poor."

Trump quotes an excerpt from Schweitzer's book: "At the center of US policy toward China was Hillary Clinton. At this critical time for US-China relations, Bill Clinton gave a number of speeches that were underwritten by the Chinese government and its supporters." Money for the speeches was then paid to the Clinton personal account while Hillary was negotiating with China on behalf of the United States. As anyone can see, there is a glaringly obvious conflict of interest as Clinton sold out the American workers, and our country, to Beijing.

Hillary Clinton has always maintained her support for the Trans-Pacific Partnership, an agreement that would cost America millions of jobs as well as its economic independence. However, since Trump has spotlighted the agreement's deficiencies and Clinton's support of it, she is now trying to walk that back, claiming she is no longer for it. However, make no mistake, Mrs. Clinton will implement the TPP agreement immediately if she is elected President, betraying the American worker once again.

Trump continues with this blistering analysis of Clinton's tenure as Secretary of State with this comment, "No Secretary of State has been more wrong, more often, and in more places than Hillary Clinton. Her decisions spread death, destruction and terrorism everywhere she touched."

"Among the victims is our late Ambassador, Chris Stevens. He was left helpless to die as Hillary Clinton soundly slept in her bed -- that's right, when the phone rang at 3 o'clock in the morning, she was sleeping," Trump contemptuously stated.

An exhaustive investigation into Benghazi and the deaths of four Americans indicates that Ambassador Stevens and his staff in Libya initiated hundreds of requests for additional security but the Hillary Clinton State Department refused every one of them.

Trump stated with no hesitation that, "She started the war that put him in Libya, denied him the security he asked for, then left him there to die (and) to cover her tracks, Hillary lied about a video being the cause of his death."

The mother of one of the victims had this to say about Hillary Clinton: "I want the whole world to know it: she lied to my face, and you don't want this person to be president."

Hillary Clinton's failure as Secretary of State is the reason we have ISIS butchering innocent people around the globe. When Hillary Clinton was sworn in as Secretary of State in 2009, things were a lot different than they are now. Libya was actually cooperating. Iraq was seeing a reduction in violence. Syria was under control and Iran was being choked by sanctions. Egypt was governed by a friendly regime that honored its peace treaty with Israel and ISIS wasn't even on the map.

When we take a look at the state of the Middle East after only four years of a Clinton State Department, we see a very different scenario. Secretary Clinton single-handedly managed to destabilize the entire Middle East while her invasion of Libya handed the country over to ISIS.

Thanks to Hillary Clinton's failures, Iran is the dominant Islamic power in the Middle East today. Thanks to Barack Obama's infamous and disastrous Iran deal, Iran will without a doubt, obtain nuclear weapons sooner than later.

Donald Trump boldly states that, "Hillary Clinton's support for violent regime change in Syria has thrown the country into one of the bloodiest civil wars anyone has ever seen – while giving ISIS a launching pad for terrorism against the West."

"Hillary Clinton forced out a friendly regime in Egypt only to replace it with the radical Muslim Brotherhood. The Egyptian military has once again regained control, but not before Clinton allowed Radical Islam to take hold in the region."

.The Obama Administration and the Clinton State department then announced a departure date for U.S. forces in Iraq. Once gone, ISIS killers were able to fill the vacuum and take over large parts of the country with ease. ISIS is only able to threaten us today because of the decisions Hillary Clinton made.

ISIS also threatens Christians and peaceful Muslims across the Middle East, and around the world. Innocent people, who only want to raise their families in peace and safety, have been terribly victimized by some of the most horrific brutality ever witnessed.

After stating the above, Donald Trump correctly implies that, "In short, Hillary Clinton's tryout for the presidency has produced one deadly foreign policy disaster after another."

To this day, Hillary Clinton refuses to seriously use the term "Radical Islamists Terrorism" and like President Obama, she will allow untold numbers of these would-be terrorist into our country under the guise of a "refugee resettlement" program.

"Hillary Clinton may be one of the most corrupt individuals to ever seek the presidency of the United States." Trump stated to an enthusiastic crowd who honored him with a standing ovation.

Trump then lays out some specifics itemized in Schweitzer's book "Clinton Cash," Things he says everyone should know and have been verified:

1. "A foreign telecom giant faced possible State Department sanctions for providing technology to Iran, and other oppressive regimes. So what did this company do? For the first time ever, they decided to pay Bill Clinton $750,000 for a single speech. The Clintons got their cash, the telecom company escaped sanctions."

2. "Hillary Clinton's State Department approved the transfer of 20% of America's uranium holdings to Russia, while 9 investors in

the deal funneled $145 million to the Clinton Foundation."

3. "Hillary Clinton appointed a top donor to a national security board with top secret access – even though he had no national security credentials."

4. "To cover-up her corrupt dealings, Hillary Clinton illegally stashed her State Department emails on a private server."

5. It has come to light that her home based email server was not only in violation of the laws that are in place to protect our most secret information from our enemies, but we now know that she deliberately disabled the key security settings on her server.

Clinton's indifference when it comes to her email server, a scandal that we all have heard about on a daily basis, further shows how she will treat the security of our nation. She is careless at best and criminal at worst. I am not sure which is a worse trait to have in a President.

Everyone involved with the set-up and security of the Clinton home-based server have plead the 5th when questioned by Congress about the issue. Currently they are all covering for her, even to their own detriment and possible prosecution. Why are so many willing to take the fall for a corrupt and possibly criminal individual as Hillary Rodham Clinton is beyond anyone's comprehension. What could she possible have on these people that they are willing to throw away their careers and lives for her?

Due to the vulnerabilities and Clinton's carelessness when it comes to her server, many nations, including Russia have made claims of hacking her system; furthermore, insinuating they have obtained the 33,000 emails that she claims to have deleted. Other hackers including the infamous and currently in custody "Guccifer" has made the same claims. And as Trump points out, it is possible that financial backers in Communist China could have them as well. This is a scenario that puts all Americans in danger.

We all know that emails are forever and most of us have been bitten by the "found" email that we never wanted discovered at one time or another; so how is it that no one can find her missing emails?

Most voters in the country find it unbelievable and suspicious that the experts working for the Obama Department of Justice and the FBI can't seem to locate them. Maybe they just don't want to find them.

Vladimir Putin assures us that he has her most confidential emails and if what he says is true, it could be a very dangerous situation for our National Security if any president were able to be blackmailed by foreign leaders.

As Donald Trump states, "We can't hand over our government to someone whose deepest, darkest secrets may be in the hands of our enemy."

Donald Trump continues to hammer Clinton on her disinterest in national security as well as her ideas on immigration security and it is apparent that Clinton is not interested in either one.

"Clinton's immigration policy will hurt the poor African-American and Hispanic workers who need jobs first; they are the ones she will hurt the most."

Trump then shares a letter his campaign received from Mary Ann Mendoza, a mother who lost her amazing son, Police Sergeant Brandon

Mendoza, after he was killed by an illegal immigrant because of the open borders policies supported by Hillary Clinton. Sadly, the Mendoza family is not the exception, as many thousands of families are suffering the same tragic fate.

Trump reads an excerpt from Mrs. Mendoza's letter:

"Hillary Clinton, who already has the blood of so many on her hands, is now announcing that she is willing to put each and every one of our lives in harms' way – an open door policy to criminals and terrorists to enter our country. Hillary is not concerned about you or I, she is only concerned about the power the presidency would bring to her. Mrs. Mendoza concluded with, "She needs to go to prison to pay for the crimes she has already committed against this country."

As Hillary Clinton stated in a recent speech, she plans to spend hundreds of billions of dollars to resettle Middle Eastern refugees in the United States. If she is allowed to do this, our country will have no money left to take care of itself. For the amount of money Hillary Clinton plans to spend on refugee resettlement, we could rebuild every inner city in America, according to Donald Trump.

"If Hillary is elected president, her immigration agenda will keep immigrant communities poor, and unemployed Americans out of work," Trump explains. "Hillary Clinton can't claim to care about the poorest communities, African-American and Hispanics, when she plans to bring in millions of new low-wage workers who will do nothing but compete against them for jobs and resources."

Whereas the Obama administration has doubled our debt, a Hillary Administration will double that number. We are already a bankrupt nation that cannot continue along this path. We must reverse this trend of spending into oblivion, so our children will not be hit with huge debt and a life that is worse than the one my generation inherited. For the first time since World War Two the inheriting generation will be left worse off than the outgoing generation. They will live under tremendous debt, few if any jobs and a national security that is virtually non-existent. We absolutely cannot do this to future generations. We owe them the chance to achieve the American Dream, not the Globalist nightmare.

Donald Trump outlined precisely what his administration will do within the first 100 days. It is an ambitious undertaking but if any man is capable of making it happen, Donald Trump is that man. Here is his agenda:

1. Appoint judges who will uphold the Constitution. Hillary Clinton's radical judges will virtually abolish the 2nd amendment.

2. Change immigration rules to give unemployed Americans an opportunity to fill good-paying jobs.

3. Stand up to countries that cheat on trade

4. Cancel agreements with countries that cheat on trade, of which there are many.

5. Cancel rules and regulations that send jobs overseas.

6. Lift restrictions on energy production.

7. Repeal and replace job-killing Obamacare.

8. Pass massive tax reform to create millions of new jobs.

9. Impose tough new ethics rules to restore dignity to the Office of Secretary of State.

"There is one common theme in all of these reforms," Donald Trump says. "It's going to be America First."

Donald Trump promises the voter that if he is elected, he will end the special interest groups in Washington D.C. and continue to expose the corrupt group of elites that have stolen America from the people of this country.

Hillary Clinton's old and tired message that "America can't change" is antithesis to Donald Trump's declaration that, "America must change."

His highly energetic speech comes just days after the firing of controversial campaign manager Corey Lewandowski and a few rocky weeks of self-inflicted wounds. Trump's campaign has been aiming to unite the Republican party and the more truths he points out and details he gives to resolving issues, the more popular he becomes with the voters.

The pundits liked what he had to say too, and below are highlights from both the left and right news groups praising the Donald Trump Speech:

Fortune: "Donald Trump Promised Us A Speech On Hillary Clinton's Past, And On Wednesday, He Didn't Disappoint." (Chris Matthews, "Trump Accuses Clinton Of Helping China In Return For Cash," Fortune, 6/22/16)

Fox News: "Donald Trump delivered a blistering attack Wednesday on Hillary Clinton's record as secretary of state, accusing the presumptive Democratic presidential nominee of milking oppressive regimes of tens of millions of dollars to benefit the Clinton Foundation -- while sleeping through her own '3 a.m. phone call' as terrorists were murdering four Americans in Libya, including Ambassador Chris Stevens." ("Trump Hammers Clinton Foreign Policy Record, Foundation Donations," Fox News, 6/22/16)

ABC News: "Presumptive Republican nominee Donald Trump today blasted Hillary Clinton as a 'world-class liar,' saying she 'may be the most corrupt person ever' to run for president." (John Santucci, Candace Smith, Paola Chavez And Veronica Stracqualursi, "Donald Trump Slams Hillary Clinton As A 'World-Class Liar'," ABC News, 6/22/16)

Slate Headline: "Trump's Speech About Hillary Was Terrifyingly Effective" (Michelle Goldberg, Slate, 6/22/16)

NPR News Headline: "Trump Just Gave The Speech Republicans Have Been Waiting 20 Years To Hear" (Mara Liasson, NPR News, 6/22/16)

CNN: "Trump: Clinton Is a 'World-Class Liar'" "[He] seemed to fuse his volatile, off-the-cuff political style with a more traditional brand of political discourse that puts reasoned arguments before voters as they make their choice for President." (Jeremy Diamond and Stephen Collinson, CNN, 6/22/16)

Bloomberg: "A Sharply Critical Speech..." "Donald Trump tied presidential rival Hillary Clinton to the 'rigged economy,' the rise of the Islamic State and government corruption in a sharply critical speech on Wednesday in Manhattan." (Kevin Cirilli, "Donald Trump Outlines His Case Against Hillary Clinton," Bloomberg, 6/22/16)

Los Angeles Times Headline: "Donald Trump Delivers Broadside Against Hillary Clinton: 'She Gets Rich Making You Poor'" (Los Angeles Times, 6/22/16)

ABC News' Tom Llamas:

Tom Llamas ✔ @TomLlamasABC

Trump gets standing o after contrasting HRC slogan "I'm with her" w/ his belief "I'm with u, the American people"

Fox News Headline: "Trump Hammers Clinton Foreign Policy Record, Foundation Donations" (Fox News, 6/22/16)

The New York Times: "Donald J. Trump delivered a scathing attack on Hillary Clinton's record on Wednesday, accusing her of being a 'world-class liar' and incompetent while trying to lay out a positive vision for America in a major speech intended to put his sputtering presidential campaign back on the offensive." (Alan Rappeport, "Donald Trump Returns Fire, Calling Hillary Clinton A 'World-Class Liar'," The New York Times, 6/22/16)

CBS News: "Donald Trump delivered a blistering rebuke of Hillary Clinton on Wednesday, attacking her actions as President Obama's secretary of state and what she did as a U.S. senator and first lady." (Rebecca Shabad,

"Donald Trump Assails 'Incompetent' Hillary Clinton In Fiery Speech," CBS News, 6/22/16)

Time: Trump's "In a speech at the Trump Soho in New York, the presumptive Republican nominee attacked Clinton's record on foreign policy and trade, arguing that her decisions were made on self-interest and unduly influenced by foreign governments. ... But while his delivery was more restrained, his attacks were as barbed as ever." (Tessa Berenson, "Donald Trump Accuses Hillary Clinton Of Corruption As Secretary Of State," Time, 6/22/16)

Mother Jones Headline: "Trump Just Gave His Sharpest Anti-Clinton Speech Yet" (Max J. Rosenthal, Mother Jones, 6/22/16)

USA Today: "Donald Trump pulled few punches in his long-planned speech blasting Hillary Clinton on everything from Iraq to Benghazi to, well, everything." (Cooper Allen, "5 Most Explosive Attacks Trump Leveled Against Clinton," USA Today, 6/22/16)

The Week Headline: "Donald Trump Tears Into Hillary Clinton During Attack Speech" (The Week, 6/22/16)

Reuters: "Donald Trump staged a harsh attack on his Democratic rival Hillary Clinton ..."arguing that, "the former secretary of state is part of a political establishment that has cheated American workers through bad trade deals and endangered U.S. national security." (Emily Flitter, "Seeking to Regain Ground, Trump Accuses Clinton of Corruption," Reuters, 6/22/16)

Donald Trump is doing exactly what we asked him to do. He is fighting with everything he has. We can't dance around the issues this election because the outcome is too important. Even if we have to cringe somewhat, remember what is at stake. Future generations are watching.

"As so often happens with Washington scandals, it isn't the original scandal that gets people in the most trouble - it's the attempted cover-up."

Tom Petri

CHAPTER 15

CLINTON SCANDALS

In Peter Schweizer's book "Clinton Cash: The Untold Story of How and Why Foreign Governments and Businesses Helped Make Bill and Hillary Rich," the Clintons are seen as a power-hungry, money-hungry, evil couple who would throw a newborn baby under the bus if it would help their pocketbook.

Once the book came out, "Clinton Cash" was quickly turned into a movie and has played for free on Breitbart.com and other outlets. To date the movie has generated more than three million views on BreitBart and if you haven't seen it already, I highly recommend you do. The level of corruption and the amounts of money that has changed hands between all of these Clinton accomplices is astounding and the people, children and elderly that they have harmed through their callous recklessness is also remarkable. How they can sleep at night is beyond me.

The following facts from Schweizer's book have been fact-checked by so many and found to be true. In fact, to date, I don't think there have been any reports of anything in the book "Clinton Cash" not being true.

1. Confirmed: Hillary's Foundation Hid a $2.35 Million Foreign Donation from the Head of the Russian Govt's Uranium Company that Had Business Before Hillary Clinton's State Dept.--a Clear Violation of the Memorandum of Understanding with the Obama Administration.

As Clinton Cash reveals, Ian Telfer, the foreign head of the Russian-owned uranium company, Uranium One, which Hillary Clinton approved to acquire U.S. uranium, made four individual hidden donations to the Clinton Foundation totaling $2.35 million, none of which appear in Clinton Foundation disclosures.

2. CONFIRMED: Bill Clinton Bagged $500,000 for a Speech in Moscow Paid for by a Kremlin-linked Bank.

The New Yorker confirms that, as Clinton Cash claims, Bill Clinton made $500,000 for a Moscow speech that was paid for by "a Russian investment bank that had ties to the Kremlin" at the time of the Uranium One deal.

3. CONFIRMED: Hillary's Brother Sits on the Board of a Mining Company that Scored an Extremely Rare "Gold Exploitation Permit" in Haiti as Hillary and Bill Clinton Disbursed Billions of U.S. Taxpayer Dollars in Haiti.

The Washington Post confirms the accuracy of Clinton Cash's revelation that Hillary Clinton's brother, Tony Rodham, serves on the board of a mining company that scored a coveted and lucrative "gold exploitation permit" in Haiti as then-Sec. of State Hillary Clinton and Bill Clinton were doling out billions of U.S. taxpayer dollars in the wake of the Haiti earthquake.

According to the Post, Rodham's mining company "won one of the first two gold-mining permits the Haitian government had issued in more than 50 years," just as Clinton Cash reveals.

4. CONFIRMED: Hillary's Foundation Hid a Foreign Donation of 2 Million Shares of Stock by a Mining Executive with Business Before

Hillary's State Dept.--a Clear Violation of the Memorandum of Understanding with the Obama Administration

The Wall Street Journal confirms the book's revelation that another foreign donation, one by Canadian mining executive Stephen Dattels, made a hidden donation of two million shares in Polo Resources that the Clinton Foundation chose not to disclose in violation of the Memorandum of Understanding the Clintons signed with the Obama administration.

5. CONFIRMED: Hillary's Approval of the Russian Takeover of Uranium One Transferred 20% of All U.S. Uranium to the Russian Govt.

The New York Times confirms, "The sale gave the Russians control of one-fifth of all uranium production capacity in the United States."

The Times also verifies the book's reporting that Hillary's uranium transfer to Russia represented, at the time, a projected 50% of all U.S. uranium output.

6. CONFIRMED: Bill Clinton was Paid by a For-Profit Education Company Laureate While the Company Benefitted from an Increase in Funding from Hillary's State Dept.

Bloomberg has confirmed that, as reported in Clinton Cash, Bill Clinton was paid by "Laureate International Universities, part of Laureate Education, Inc," a position he abruptly resigned from recently.

Bloomberg's examination confirms that "in 2009, the year before Bill Clinton joined Laureate, the nonprofit received 11 grants worth $9 million from the State Department or the affiliated USAID. In 2010, the group received 14 grants worth $15.1 million. In 2011, 13 grants added up to $14.6 million. The following year, those numbers jumped: They received 21 grants worth $25.5 million, including a direct grant from the State Department."

Neither the company nor the Clintons will release the exact amounts Bill received for working for the controversial for-profit education company.

7. CONFIRMED: The Clinton Foundation has Been Forced to Re-file at Least 5 Years of Annual Tax Returns and May Audit Other Clinton Foundation Returns

Reuters has confirmed that "Hillary Clinton's family's charities are re-filing at least five annual tax returns" as "the foundation and its list of donors have been under intense scrutiny."

8. CONFIRMED: At Least $26 Million of the Clintons' Wealth Comes from Speaking Fees by Companies and Organizations that are also major Clinton Foundation Donors

The Washington Post has confirmed in an article based on Clinton Cash that, according to the Post's independent analysis, "Bill Clinton was paid more than $100 million for speeches between 2001 and 2013, according to federal financial disclosure forms filed by Hillary Clinton during her years as a senator and as secretary of state."

Of that, reports the Post, "Bill Clinton was paid at least $26 million in speaking fees by companies and organizations that are also major donors to the foundation he created after leaving the White House, according to a Washington Post analysis of public records and foundation date.

9. CONFIRMED: Bill Clinton Delivered Numerous Speeches Paid for By Individuals and Corporations with Pending Business Before Hillary's State Dept.

ABC News has confirmed Clinton Cash's reporting that myriad businesses and individuals paid Bill Clinton to deliver speeches even as their companies had business on Sec. of State Hillary Clinton's desk.

"Records supported the premise that former President Clinton accepted speaking fees from numerous companies and individuals with interests pending before the State Department," reported ABC News.

10. CONFIRMED: Bill Clinton Lied about Hosting a Meeting with Frank Giustra and Kazakh Nuclear Officials at Clinton's Home in Chappaqua, New York.

New York Times Pulitzer Prize-winning investigative reporter Jo Becker confirmed in a one-hour Fox News television special on Clinton Cash that Bill Clinton lied when questioned about whether Clinton, Giustra, and executives from the Kazakh-owned nuclear company Kazatomprom ever met in Clintons' home.

"When I first contacted both the Clinton Foundation--Mr. Clinton's spokesman--and Mr. Giustra, they denied any such meeting ever took place," said Becker.

"And then when we told them, 'Well we already talked to the head of Kazatomprom, who not only told us all about the meeting, but actually has a picture of him and Bill at the home in Chappaqua, and that he proudly displayed it on his office wall.' They then acknowledged that yes, the meeting had taken place.[29]"

11. CONFIRMED: Clinton Cash author, Peter Schweizer, is Currently Conducting a Deep Dive Investigative Report on Republican Presidential Candidate Jeb Bush's Financial Dealings

"The wide-ranging examination will appraise the possible 2016 contenders involvement in Florida real estate deals, an airport deal that involved state funds while Bush was Florida's chief executive, and Chinese investments in Bush's private equity funds," reports CBS News.

The Hillary Clinton campaign continues to struggle in its efforts to spin and distract from the growing pile of Clinton Cash facts mainstream media outlets have already confirmed and verified are correct.

Some other well known things about Bill and Hillary Clinton are below. If you are my age or older, then you remember some of these things; but if you are a millennial, you are likely hearing them for the first time.

As soon as Hillary Clinton became America's first lady and gained national and world-wide prominence, she has been embroiled in scandal after scandal. Admittedly, some were caused by her husband; however, as she has continued to make a name for herself as a political heavyweight, controversy continues to hang over her head.

Pundits on both sides of the aisle continue to worry about her ability to take this to the next level. Past scandals and now more recent controversy involving her health are making those who support her extremely nervous. Clinton admits that using a private server was not the best thing to do, but she still maintains that she did nothing wrong. Even as the missing emails trickle in from obscurity, miraculously found either through a really talented geek, or more than likely someone had them a long time ago because they hacked her extremely vulnerable server before Clinton had the opportunity to delete them.

Cropping up now are lingering and quite serious questions about suspicious donations made to Clinton's foundation.

A conservative news site, WND recently published a list of "Hillary's 22 biggest scandals ever,[30]" which includes some things you know and some things you don't. The Clinton crime family goes way back but it needs to stop with this election. Some of their transgressions are as follows

:

1. The Clintons turned the IRS into a 'Gestapo' during Bill Clinton's second term in

office. Reports surfaced that prominent conservative groups had been subjected to audits while there was no indication that any corresponding organizations on the political left had been targeted by the IRS.

2. Hillary Clinton would cover Bill's dirty deeds even amid allegations of sexual assault against Bill Clinton during his presidency. The charges cast a negative light on not only Bill, but Hillary, too. So as the political power couple they were, and still are, Hillary reportedly aided her husband not only by publicly defending him, but by using shady and potentially criminal tactics in an effort to de-legitimize his many accusers.

3. The Clintons' were caught looting the White House after Clinton's second term came to a close. The couple reportedly attempted to take roughly $190,000 worth of furniture and other items from the White House in addition to causing about $14,000 in damages to the presidential mansion. They were forced to bring the stolen items backs.

4. File-gate: The Clintons reportedly gained confidential tax records on many of their political rivals, a scheme in which Judicial Watch claimed Hillary played a central role.

5. Hillary's top juggernaut Huma Abedin, a confidant who served as Hillary Clinton's deputy chief of staff, was linked to the Muslim Brotherhood specifically through the al-Qaeda connections of both her mother and father.

6. The 1993 suspicious death of family friend and White House counsel Vince Foster links back to the Clintons. Foster was embroiled in at least a few of the Clintons' early scandals and was still involved until the day he died. Initially ruled a suicide, the circumstances of Foster's death have led to significant speculation in the decades since.

7. Email-gate: One of the more recent scandals involves Hillary Clinton's admitted use of a personal email server to share official correspondences during her stint as secretary of state. We all know the details and we all know she intentionally broke the law. She should not be

running for president, she should be going to prison for this one.

8. China-gate: Sale of high-tech secrets: Judicial Watch initially released a report suggesting Chinese corporations supported Bill Clinton's 1996 reelection effort in exchange for technology secrets.

9. Travel-gate: Always room for friends during the Clinton administration. The Clintons reportedly laid off the White House travel office staff so that they could fill the department with family members and friends. Nepotism at its finest.

10. Whitewater: One of the most identifiable Clinton scandals involved an investigation into a real estate deal that later encompassed accusations of improper campaign donations and the couple's potential involvement in Foster's death.

11. 'Landing under sniper fire' in Bosnia: Hillary Clinton has faced criticism for her since-debunked 2008 claim that, more than a decade earlier, she was touring war-torn Bosnia in a helicopter as it sustained sniper fire. While she

described a very dramatic landing, news footage of the event showed no such threat existed.

12. Hillary's 'missing' law firm billing records: More than 100 pages of pertinent information went missing ahead of a 1994 federal investigation into Hillary Clinton's involvement in the Whitewater scandal. When the documents did surface two years later it was revealed that her fingerprints were on the documents and that they had been in her house the entire time.

13. Pardon-gate: The wife of one convicted tax cheat pardoned by Bill Clinton at the end of his second term responded in kind by becoming a major contributor to Hillary's 2000 campaign to become a New York senator.

14. Hillary's cash cows and 9,987 percent profit: A series of investments in cattle futures was seriously profitable for a young Hillary Clinton. Between 1978 and 1979, a $1,000 investment turned into a nearly $100,000 profit, a success subsequently linked to a Clinton supporter who also happened to be a high-level player at Tyson Foods. Insider-Trading?

15. Clinton body count: Vince Foster was not the only suspicious death linked to the Clintons. In addition to those who met an untimely end after crossing the powerful couple, many others on their wrong side also ended up behind bars.

16. Reports indicate community organizer and author of Rules for Radicals, Saul Alinsky, was a major influence on a young Hillary Clinton. She was involved in Alinsky's group, Industrial Areas Foundation, for decades after the radical activist's death. She is still a fan of his today.

17. Audio unveiled decades after it was recorded revealed Hillary Clinton celebrating the fact that an accused child rapist she represented was set free in 1975 – despite the fact that she insinuated that she believed him to be guilty of the crime. A lot of us will remember hearing her cackle over that one.

18. Hillary ca$hes in: Iranian fund-raising" The Clinton Foundation reportedly received numerous financial contributions from a group

accused of serving as an agent of the Iranian government.

19. Clinton Foundation: The Clintons' nonprofit organization has faced controversy far beyond the Iranian connection, including accusations of tax fraud and a secretive deal believed to have facilitated the release of nuclear material to Russia.

20. Benghazi: Four American lives lost: A scandal that continues to incite passions involves then-Secretary of State Hillary Clinton, lambasted for her perceived inaction before, during, and after a 2012 attack that killed four Americans in Libya; further incensing everyone with her lies and misrepresentation of the facts. Clinton lied to America without any remorse at all.

21. Peter Franklin Paul: Hillary's friend goes to prison. Paul was an entertainment executive and major financial supporter of Hillary Clinton's 2000 Senate bid. He has since become an outspoken critic after accepting a plea deal and serving three years in prison for what he contended was retaliation for calling attention to fraud within

Clinton's fund-raising methods. Friends shouldn't cross the Clinton Clan.

22. Watergate: A Liar Fired. As a House Judiciary Committee staffer in 1974, Hillary Clinton helped investigate the Watergate scandal that led to Richard Nixon's resignation. She was soon fired by a supervisor who described her as an "unethical, dishonest lawyer."

There are entire books written about the Clinton scandals out there and if is frightening when you start perusing them to find out how horrible these Clintons really are. There is nothing they will not do to live in the White House again. Even with all the baggage she carries, it is unbelievable that the Democrats are allowing her to run, much less putting their globalist aspirations on her shoulders. In a sensible world someone like Hillary Clinton would never make it out of the gate, much less to the finish line. But these times are different and if a businessman turned politician can sweep the Republican Primaries to win by a larger margin than ever before, then this old woman named Hillary Clinton has a chance, too.

"The United States can't keep a completely open system if the rest of the world is less open. The United States may have to take a leaf out of the book of Japan, China, and Germany, and have protectionism inside the system."

Robert Mundell

CHAPTER 16

PROTECTIONISM

Protectionism is the economic policy of restricting trade between countries through methods like tariffs, enforcing strict quotas, and a variety of other regulations, all designed to force fair trade and competition between both imports and exports. By design, the protectionist policies protect the businesses and jobs of a country by limiting trade with foreign nations.

During our "free trade" years the government (composed of many administrations) forgot that free trade was supposed to be equitable. The trade imbalance for America is so great in 2016, that it is laughable to even say the word "free trade". During the years that lead to the crisis we are now in, protectionism, like nationalism, became a word that represents hate and discrimination. It is one of those words "we dare not say" or risk being called all kinds of names and accused of everything from hating Muslims, Blacks, Gays, Women, Men, Criminals, to even hating your own mother. The liberals have been very successful in demonizing anyone who believes that America needs to return to the qualities of protectionism, even ruining people's lives who disagree with their agenda. The liberal left has become divisive but their tactics are transparent. They intend to divide and conquer but the popular anti-globalism and anti-immigration movements continue to grow in numbers. The people of America see what is taking place in the rest of the world and now our globalist politicians have come forward and stated that their agenda is in fact, "Globalism and the New World Order". The people of America and all around the world are beginning to understand and they are demanding that everyone just "halt in their tracks."

Sometimes you have to stop and take another look around. Make sure that the path you are one is still the one you want to be on.

According to the Real Clear Politics[31] taken in early August show that a majority of Americans, a whopping 64% of them, feel like the country is on the wrong track and they are willing to give Donald Trump a chance to see what he can do because we already know how badly the establishment politicians have done.

It is time to give the unknown a chance. Donald Trump is a proven success in his business and family. Many Americans feel that he can do the same for our country so they are pledging their vote to the man who wants to put America First. And if that means protectionism, nationalism, Americanism or any other "ism" you want to put on it, Donald Trump is going to rebuild our country, our spirit and our hope.

"These fallen heroes represent the character of a nation who has a long history of patriotism and honor - and a nation who has fought many battles to keep our country free from threats of terror."

Michael N. Castle

CHAPTER 17

COMBATING ISIS
RADICAL ISLAMIC TERRORISM

On June 15, 2016, Donald Trump gave an important speech about our nation's lack of foreign policy and he laid out his plan to defeat ISIS. With the ever growing threat of terrorism attacking on our soil and the world around us, it is more important than ever that we have a Commander in Chief that understands the enemy and can say its name - "Radical Islamic Terrorism."

In Europe we have witnessed even more bloodshed and carnage as the attacks are becoming a daily occurrence across the once beautiful continent. Terrorism is also killing the tourist industries in France, Brussels, Germany, Italy and Great Britain as the threats of torture and death are real.

Donald Trump vows to stop the hateful ideology of radical Islam and their oppression of Gays, Women, Christians and other Muslims.

The rise of Isis is the direct result of policy decisions made by President Barack Obama and the former Secretary of State, Hillary Clinton with the reckless way they pulled out of Iraq. Obama and Clinton gave the decimated Al Qaida a safe little vacuum with which to grow and it sprang forth new life and began to spread throughout the region. ISIS grew from a "JV team" (Obama's word) to the religious war they are today. They want world domination and they won't stop until they have achieved it.

ISIS went from controlling and/or inhabiting only a handful of countries in 2015 to a substantially higher number of countries influenced today in 2016. President Obama would have you think that ISIS is still a minor player but we all know that isn't the truth.

ISIS is currently trying to infiltrate the U.S. through Europe and we will have large numbers of ISIS fighters in our nation very shortly, if not already. Their intention is clear with their chants of "Death to America" and only a fool, like Hillary Clinton and Barack Obama would continue to march on when told a bomb is lying up ahead.

Russia also has a huge problem with ISIS, and Trump and Putin plan to work together to disable and destroy ISIS. They will shut down their Internet access for recruiting, therefore shutting down their capacity to grow. Then they will annihilate ISIS, but the fight is not limited to them. Al Qaeda, also will be starved of funding and the line which draws back to Hamas and Hezbollah will be exposed and through this methodology, they too, will be starved into civility.

As we know, civility is not the concern of most Muslims. They are raised with this deep-seated hate since knee high and even moderate Muslims will stand with their radical friends should the need arise.

9/11, the Ford Hood Shooting, The San Bernardino attack, The Orlando Attack, The Boston Bomber were all crimes perpetrated by the offspring of migrants.

Trump tells the people, "We should only admit into this country those who respect our values." Trump calls this extreme vetting like none we have ever seen before. Screening out not only those with radical beliefs but also those with possible ties to anyone with radical beliefs.

Trump states that VISAs will temporarily be stopped from particular hot spots until such time as vetting can take place, while Hillary Clinton wants to increase and fast-track the flow of immigrants from these same hot spots without any vetting or knowledge of who they are. This will cost our nation about $400 billion dollars and will leave an untold number of molested children in its wake.

With Trump's promise to restore common sense to the process for securing our nation, we should be able to quickly sweep the country and get out those here illegally.

Americans are tired of being the victim of the illegal immigrants, political correctness, and politicians who pander to the different fascist groups. We want our country safe and we want to know that radical Islam has been exterminated and not encouraged.

With determination we should be able to destroy ISIS and restore the world to an imperfect yet relatively harmonious place to live.

Trump agrees that we will be able to accomplish our goals if we work together with other nations who are also concerned about the safety of their citizens. We will expose and rip out each terrorist group, destroying them on site; viciously, if necessary.

We will fight fire with fire and will not stop until the threat of Radical Islamist Terrorism is gone. We will restore pride in our values, our history, and our future for the citizens of the

United States and the world over. We will restore our country and the bond we all share through our struggles with daily life. We have to show the world that America is strong and we will persevere. We have to show them that we are still the best and we will rise again through our unity.

Renewing the spirit of Americanism will help heal our country by emphasizing what we have in common, not what pulls us apart.

Trump's pledge to America is this: "As your President, I will be your single greatest champion. I will fight to insure that every American is treated equally, protected equally and honored equally. We will reject bigotry and hatred and oppression in all of its many ugly forms, and seek a new future built on our common culture of values as one American people. Only this way, will we make America Great again and safe again for everyone.[32]"

"When the power of love overcomes the love of power, the world will know peace."

Jimi Hendrix

CHAPTER 18

THE WAR MUST END

"I care too much about my country to let this happen." Donald J. Trump, June 16, 2016.

Donald Trump was supposed to have another one of his exciting rallies tonight. The people of West Bend, WI. had their tickets in hand and were waiting to hear his encouraging words of hope and strength. But in light of the recent rioting taking place in Milwaukee, Wisconsin, Trump took the opportunity to speak to the people of America. giving an amazing policy speech (yes, using a teleprompter) on "How to make America Safe Again."

The events in Milwaukee have become an epidemic in our country as George Soros funds the growth of the group called Black Lives Matter. Their purpose is to cause mass destruction and riots in the streets of America and now across the world, in an effort to intimidate and cause harm.

Since the now infamous "Stand Your Ground" death of Trayvon Martin in Florida and the subsequent acquittal of accused George Zimmerman, black America has become very angry because of what they perceive as the persecution of black people by white America and especially by the police. This anti-police, anti-white group has taken the name of Black Lives Matters and through social media, the small, insignificant group of angry blacks has turned into an international terrorist organization, causing significant property damage and even loss of life.

Recent riots have taken place in Ferguson, Missouri over the Mike Brown death; Baltimore, Maryland over the Freddie Brown death; Staten Island, NY over the Eric Garner death; and now in Milwaukee, Wisconsin over the death of Sylville Smith. This group concentrates its efforts not on the outrageous numbers of black on black violence, murder, and abortion, but instead on the white on black crime. They especially love it if a police officer kills a black criminal and that police officer is white.

In Ferguson, late on the evening of Nov. 24, 2014, the announcement came that the grand jury would not indict Officer Darren Wilson for the

August 9, 2014 death of Michael Brown. Whether you agree or not with this decision, the city of Ferguson and cities across the U.S., including Chicago, Los Angeles, Atlanta, New York, and Boston were hit with violent protest and they continued four nights in a row. While some people did have peaceful protests in Ferguson, the majority got violent; setting fire to police cars, looted businesses, and destroying buildings and property.

In Baltimore, Maryland angry residents took to the streets of northwest Baltimore to protest another death of a black man at the hands of police. Freddie Gray, the 25-year-old African American who died on April 19, 2015 from a severe spinal cord injury suffered while in police custody. He was arrested for having an illegal switchblade according to police reports, and while in the back of the police van, he sustained injuries that put him in a coma.

The officers involved were charged with homicide on May 1, 2015, by the Baltimore City State's Attorney, Marilyn Mosby. She declared that the officers were negligent when they failed to strap Gray in after placing him under arrest; that they caused him to be thrown around, thus sustaining his fatal injuries. The officers were indicted on May 21, 2015 and two stood trial and were acquitted. The others are expected to follow. .

Protest erupted from the minute Freddie Gray was hospitalized and continued even after the indictment was handed down.

Governor Larry Hogan declared a state of emergency, called in the National Guard, and set a curfew as demonstrators threw rocks and cinder blocks at police and firefighters, looted stores, and set buildings and cars on fire. Fifteen police officers were injured.

On August 13, 2016, Milwaukee, Wisconsin, responded to the fatal shooting of 23-year-old Sylville Smith by police. It didn't take long for the screams of police brutality to begin by BLM and the New Black Panthers. The facts were not even in but the protesters had already decided to riot.

Sylville Smith was well known to the police with numerous misdemeanors on his record. This particular day, Mr. Smith also had a weapon; a stolen semi-automatic pistol and he was brandishing it as he ran from the car at a traffic stop. Two officers pursued on foot after him and ordered him twice to put down the weapon. Smith refused and was shot twice in the pursuit; once in the arm and once in the chest. He died on the scene and his buddy was apprehended and is in custody.

The riots began immediately and then it was revealed that the officer was also a black man and a school chum of Mr. Smith's, but that didn't curtail the violence, instead it escalated it.

It was reported that black mobs were seeking out white people to harm and one group dragged a white woman from her car and beat her up.

The sister of the dead man, Sherelle Smith, was seen on camera telling the rioters to move to the suburbs. Burn down the suburbs.

"Burning down sh*t ain't gonna help nothin'," yells Sherelle Smith. "You're burnin' down sh*t we need in our community."

"Take that sh*t to the suburbs. Burn that sh*t down!" she demands.[33]

With Milwaukee, the violence against Americans has escalated and before long, it will make its way through the heartland of America. We will be forced to either back down and let them have our homes and our lives, and conform to their ways or we will have to fight back. We can't let thugs like BLM, George Soros, and Hillary

Clinton take-over our country. And that is the point Donald Trump was making today.

Riots like these must stop and President Obama has to step up and say, "Enough. Our police must be respected and law and order must prevail in our society, all societies, in order to survive."

However, we all know that Obama is not going to say any of that. He will grab his clubs and play another round of golf.

These riots are going to continue until the day Obama is out of office. The question is, "How many of us will have to suffer before that day arrives?"

Donald Trump's speech today was presidential and forceful. He made it clear that when he becomes President, this lawless behavior will stop. We can all feel safe again and we can raise our children knowing that they will have a future. Donald Trump will never stop fighting for the people and he will never stop fighting for America.

If you didn't see his entire speech, it is on You Tube and it is worth a watch.[34]

"It takes two to speak
the truth: one to speak,
and another to hear."

Henry David Thoreau

CHAPTER 19

I SPEAK THE TRUTH

The speech that pivoted Donald Trump from boisterous primary candidate to a first class Presidential general election candidate was delivered to a energetic crowd in Charlotte, North Carolina on June 18, 2016. It was a speech that has the elites and Hillary Clinton quaking in their boots.

Rudy Giuliani did an amazing job with his smack down of Hillary Clinton. He focused on her carelessly dangerous behavior with our national security secrets and he explains that based on her history, she would be unable to pass a background check and as he says, "Is this someone we want to hand our country over to?"

To a raucous and cheering crowd, Rudy Giuliani introduced Donald J. Trump, hopefully our 45th President.

Trump took the stage to thunderous applause and the crowd chanted "Trump, Trump, Trump."

He began with taking a moment to reflect on the heartbreak and devastation in Baton Rouge,

415

Louisiana, caused by the recent floods. Louisiana is a state that Trump claims is very special to him.

"We are all one nation. When one state hurts, we all hurt. And we must all work together to lift each other up. Working, building, restoring together. Our prayers are with the families who have lost loved ones and we send them our deepest condolences."

"Though words cannot express the sadness that one feels at times like this, I hope everyone in Louisiana knows that our country is praying for them and standing with them to help them in these difficult hours, they are very, very difficult. Thank you. We are one country, one people and we will have together one great, fantastic future." As Trump spoke the crowds exploded in cheers and applause.

"Together I'd like to talk about the new American future that we are going to create as a team together." Trump told the crowd.

Donald Trump proceeded to reiterate his plan for bringing back jobs, securing our border and restoring our nation.

Last week Trump laid out his plan for bringing back jobs to our country. It was an amazingly detailed plan that even the most hard-core anti-Trumpers could find little, if anything, to complain about.

Then a few days later he laid out a plan to defeat Radical Islamic Terrorism; another inspiring speech on how he will protect our nation.

Condemning the violence in our streets, Donald Trump praised our Police Officers and Law Enforcement Officers who have sacrificed so greatly in these very difficult times and ensured them that he will stand by them and that law and order will be reestablished in our country.

"Every single citizen in our land has the right to live in safety, to be one united nation. We must protect all of our people - all of our people! But we must also provide opportunities for all of our people. We cannot make America Great Again if we leave any community behind."

Trump speaks passionately about the nearly 4 in 10 African American children living in poverty; promising that a Trump Administration will not rest until "children of every color in this country are fully included in the American Dream. Jobs, safety and opportunity is what we have to have and it is what we need. Fair and equal representation."

"This is what I promise to African Americans, Hispanics, Americans of all types, of all colors. of all religions, this is what we promise, we all promise, everybody in this room promises. This is what we have to do."

Those of us who have watched Donald Trump since June 16, 2015 are sitting in awe, speechless at this new Donald Trump.

"But to achieve this new American future, we must break from the failures of the past," then Trump reminds us all that he is not a politician, he is a businessman; he's created jobs, and he's a builder. He never wanted to learn the language of the insider and he never wanted to be politically correct because it takes far too much time and causes a multitude of other issues.

Then Donald Trump took a more humble tone and expressed his regret for anything he may have done in the primary that seemed distasteful to some or may have caused personal pain.

"Sometimes, in the heat of debate and speaking on a multitude of issues, you don't choose the right words or you say the wrong thing. I have done that,(long pause while the crowd chuckled) and believe it or not, I regret it. And I do regret it particularly where it may have caused personal pain," Trump said. "Too much is at stake for us to be consumed with these issues. But one thing I can promise you is this: I will always tell you the truth."

"I speak the truth for all of you and for everyone in this country who doesn't have a voice, of which there are many. I speak the truth on behalf of the factory worker who lost his or her job and that's happening more and more in our country.

"I speak the truth on behalf of the Veteran who is being denied the care they need and the medical care they deserve and so many are not making it but they are going to make it if Trump becomes president. That I can tell you."

"I speak the truth on behalf of the family living near the border that deserves to be safe in their own country but is instead living with no security and no protection at all." The crowd went wild chanting "Build That Wall, Build That Wall." Trumps proudly smiled and said, "We will build the wall. Believe me. We will build the wall."

Then he spoke to all the people who feel that they have been forgotten with no one listening to them yet they are forced to watch as insiders fight only for other insiders and not for them.

Americans are angry on so many levels. The poverty, the unemployment, the failing schools, the jobs moving to other countries, "I am fighting for these forgotten Americans."

Trump told the crowd that he is deeply proud and humbled that they have placed so much trust in him and he promised to continue to work every day to keep his promise to America and to repay the loyalty that so many have placed in him. Donald Trump knows what is at stake in this election, he knows, as do most, that we are in the fight for our lives, together, to save our country.

Trump talks about our young people who are denied the American Dream. Trump realizes that the entire country loses when "Children of limitless potential are denied the opportunities to contribute their talents because we failed to provide them the opportunities that they deserve. Let our children be 'Dreamers' too."

Trump spoke more about our failed government, promising the crowd, and everyone watching, that he will always place America First.

Then he promises the crowd that he will never lie to them, he will never stop fighting for them. The American People are his only interest. For a country that has been so good to him, he is giving back now. He is self-funding his own campaign because now it is about the American People.

Then he called on Hillary Clinton to apologize to the American people for all of her many transgressions, lies and criminal activities; some of which have lead to destruction, terrorism, and to the deaths of Americans.

He called on Obama to apologize to the American people for his lies as well, like "If you like your Doctor, you can keep your Doctor.[35]"

Donald Trump has proven with this speech and others that he has the demeanor to be the president. He is calm, effective and proving more every day that he has what it takes to set this nation back on the right track. The more people see him, the more they like him.

"Never believe that a few caring people can't change the world. For, indeed, that's all who ever have."

Margaret Mead

CHAPTER 20

TRUMP CARES

On August 19, 2016, Donald Trump went to Baton Rouge, Louisiana to see firsthand the destruction caused by the weekend's floods then later in the afternoon, he held a rally in Dimondale, Michigan.

Baton Rouge was hit with historic flooding when 21.86 inches of rain fell in Livingston, Louisiana, according to National Weather Service; while gauges in other areas like Watson, Louisiana measured more than 31 inches. That staggering amount of rain left several rivers flooded far beyond the record breaking level from 33 years ago. The flood was severe and thousands of homes were damaged by its truly historic proportions. At least five people died while many others lost everything.

Louisiana Governor John Bel Edwards told the press that officials "Won't know the death toll for sure for several more days."

Donald Trump, accompanied by his Vice Presidential pick, Governor Mike Pence, went to see for himself. He also brought with him an 18-wheeler full of supplies for the victims of the flooding and helped unload with the other volunteers.

"To the people of Louisiana: We are with you and will always be with you." Trump said.

Louisiana flood victims were thrilled to greet Donald Trump and Mike Pence. In spite of the conditions, Trump was greeted like a rock star. He even signed some hats.

Trump said, as for the people he met during his visit in Louisiana, "Their spirit will overcome."

President Barack Obama signed a disaster declaration for the state, providing federal aid to support recovery efforts, but he did that from his vacation in Martha's Vineyard. He never left the golf course and Hillary Clinton is there as well celebrating her husband's birthday. They are huddled up partying while Trump is hands-on helping the relief efforts.

Trump took a jab at Obama while there, successfully shaming the president into going to the flood zone by telling the crowd that, "Obama ought to get off the golf course, and get down there."

Obama, and I presume Hillary Clinton, will make their way to Baton Rouge eventually, but in the meantime, there is seafood to eat, champagne to drink, and globalism to discuss. Their plates are kind of full. Their nonchalant attitude is worse than even George Bush's during Hurricane Katrina; but yet, the media will give them a pass.

Former Senator Mary Landrieu (D-LA), a supporter of Hillary Clinton's, surprised everyone with her praise of Donald Trump for coming to Louisiana during the floods. Landrieu said, "I hope Secretary Clinton will make her way down; I hope President Obama will make a visit."

Landrieu understands that a visit from the GOP candidate brings awareness and money to the state and that is something they need right now.

She added, "I want to thank Mr. Trump for coming to Louisiana. I think the Governor's admonition about not using it as a press op is a good one, but he brought attention to our state, and we need that now, because, this disaster, Brianna, is far larger than people can appreciate on television."

Later in the day, Trump held a rally in Dimondale and it was poignant and respectful.

Donald Trump asked the people "Are you ready to vote for an honest government?" The crowd rose to their feet cheering.

Trump promised the people that a Trump administration will end the corruption and restore integrity to government service.

"I will work for you, and I will work for no one else, I will work for you. I will never lie to you, I will never put any other interest before you and I will never, ever stop fighting for you." Donald Trump informed the crowd that the government will start working for the people again.

"We have a divided country. It's totally divided. The era of division will be replaced by a future of unity, total unity. We will love each other. We will have one country, everybody will work together."

"We are going to do it by emphasizing what we all have in common as Americans, it is time to break with the failures of the past and to fight for every last child in this country to have the better future they deserve."

"The changes I promise to all of you, an honest government, with low taxes, a thriving economy and a just society for each and every

American. It's time to vote for a new American future. Together, we will make America wealthy again. We will make America united again., We will make America proud again. We will make America safe again and we will Make America Great again."

In the past week, Donald Trump has undergone a personality shift. He has stopped his bombastic, loud, in your face, rhetoric and taken on the role of a President.

Trump told people at the beginning of his campaign that a shift would come when the time was right and I guess he determined that time is now. His pivot has been met with indignation and fear from #NeverTrumpers but the rest of the country is seeing a new Donald Trump. He is full of confidence and ready to get started on the job. Who needs to wait for an election, just let him get to work. That is his attitude and millions upon millions of loyal and dedicated patriots agree with him.

Donald Trump flies into Baton Rouge, Louisiana a presidential candidate and he flew out looking and sounding like President Donald J. Trump.

"Personal transformation can and does have global effects. As we go, so goes the world, for the world is us. The revolution that will save the world is ultimately a personal one."

Marianne Williamson

CHAPTER 21

AN AMAZING TRANSFORMATION

Donald Trump has spent the last week transforming his campaign into a first rate movement. He has delivered one explosive rally and speech after another. It seems like he just miraculously woke up one morning, jumped out of bed and pivoted.

We all watched with baited breath through the primary campaign to see what outrageous thing Donald Trump would say next. Die-hard supporters would cringe and do the "face-palm" with every incident but even as Trump said his worst, he didn't seem to lose many votes.

Donald Trump's campaign is very similar to that of Barack Obama's (please don't yell at your book). Donald Trump and Barack Obama were both newcomers to the scene.

Obama was new to the Senate in spite of being raised and groomed for politics; he was still a relative nobody when he launched his extraordinarily successful campaign.

Obama came out of nowhere and beat the Clinton Machine in an embarrassing loss for Hillary Clinton. She never saw it coming, causing some of us to feel a wee bit bad for her; just a bit.

Donald Trump, even though he is well known throughout the world is new to politics too, but he has gone from a 1% chance of winning to the amazing campaign he has built. Donald Trump should be nothing but proud of everything he has done so far.

The past week he has given a significant speech every day. They are no longer the typical fun-filled rally of laughs and cheers but are now fun-filled information packed speeches with specifics on his agenda and plans.

His total agenda is pro-American. He will negotiate fair and balanced trade deals, repeal Obama's handy-work and rebuild our nation. He wants to take care of our vets, elderly, young and everyone in between.

And unlike President Barack Obama, Donald Trump constantly praises our men and women in blue, "I want to thank all of those in our police departments all over our country and our law enforcement community."

Donald Trump has spent the week making a personal plea to African Americans. He speaks from the heart when he details the devastation that the Obama agenda has had on the black youth of our country. They have the highest unemployment rate and if Hillary Clinton brings in all the refugees she wants to, their unemployment numbers will skyrocket. Black communities all across the nation will suffer tremendously at the hands of Hillary Clinton and the Globalists. Donald Trump implores them to get out and vote for him because he wants to save the youth, no matter the color; Donald Trump wants to be their advocate.

I have watched this past week, spellbound, by the dramatic change I have seen in Donald Trump. He has had my support since day one, but in recent months I have had to shake my head more times than I care to admit; but this week I have seen Donald Trump grow into the position he is running for. He understands unity and he wants an inclusive country and an inclusive party."

At a rally today on August 20, 2016 in Fredericksburg, Virginia, Donald Trump delivered a powerful and very presidential speech to a room filled with love and respect.

"My goal is to provide every African America child in our country with access to the ladder of American success. That means good education and a great paying job. It includes also school choice (and) competition. It means reforming regulations so young Americans can get the credit they need to start a small business and that includes African Americans, Hispanics and everybody else in our country. That's what we need. It means trade and immigration policies that put American workers at the front of the line, way ahead of the workers of other countries who are beating us so badly. They are beating us so badly.

"Hillary Clinton's amnesty plan will give jobs, benefits, and social security to millions of people who are here illegally at taxpayer expense and many of these people are treated better than our vets are treated. That is not going to happen."

Trump continued, "Her plan would bring 620,000 refugees in her first term alone, from Syria. Not going to know who they are or where they will come from. Could be the great Trojan horse of all time. Get ready. Get ready."

Trump states that, "She (Hillary Clinton) would rather provide a job to a refugee living overseas than a young, unemployed African American youth in Virginia. A Trump Administration will put American workers first."

"Americanism, not globalism will be our credo. We will bring America together as one country again, united as Americans in common purpose and common dreams. We will have a thriving economy, a strong border, a powerful military, a peaceful nation, a rising standard of living. This is what I promise you. Let's get out there and win on November 8th."

Donald Trump concluded his omnipotent speech with this, "We are going to win in the state of Virginia. If we win in the state of Virginia, we are going to the White House and we are going to take care of our people. We are going for victory, we must win on November 8th. Together, we will make America wealthy again, we will make America proud again, we will make America safe again. And We Will Make America Great Again for each and every American. Thank you and God Bless You.[36]"

Donald Trump has stumped the press, delighted his supporters and from watching his Twitter feed, he has picked up roughly 200,000 new Twitter followers in the past ten days alone. I would say he has had a phenomenal couple of weeks and there is a lot to be hopeful for.

"In this life, we have to make many choices. Some are very important choices. Some are not. Many of our choices are between good and evil. The choices we make, however, determine to a large extent our happiness or our unhappiness, because we have to live with the consequences of our choices."

James E. Faust

CHAPTER 22

EPILOGUE
THE CHOICE

This 2016 election is most definitely a history making moment for our great nation. We have a choice to make; one that will inevitably alter the lives of our children and grandchildren forever.

For the first time since I became a voter, Americans will have to make a clear and concise decision on the path our country will follow. It would seem to most to be an easy decision; however, there are some who still struggle with the question.

With the current leadership, the vacancy left by Justice Antonin Scalia, as well as the ever-growing population of illegals invading our borders, it is perhaps the most important election of our time. Our country's future hangs in the balance and we must decide once and for all whether we will remain a sovereign nation that serves its own people, or whether we irrevocably turn toward a globalist, borderless society that regards humans as merely a means to an end to serve the United Nations and it's ruthless, power-hungry leaders.

Donald Trump understands this choice and has made it a focal point in his campaign. In Donald Trump we have found an advocate not only for America, but for the world as a whole. He understands that unless the United States once again becomes the leader of the free world, then the world will suffer as well.

Our country needs a forceful leader. Without one at the helm, America will be forever diminished and America's downfall will be the downfall of civilized society all over the world.

Trump has said that our trade imbalances with almost every single nation on the planet must be reversed. We are currently losing so much money every year under Obama and the current traitorous House and Senate, that if we don't reverse course and right this ship now, it will sink faster than the Titanic and the people of America will drown.

Our immigration and foreign policies have run amok and must be changed to protect the interest of the American worker and our nation. In the words of Donald Trump, we must now take the attitude of "America First." We must now choose between Nationalism and Globalism.

In Barack Obama and Hillary Clinton, we have two committed globalists, who are determined to remove our borders and surrender our nation to the control of foreign interests. As ardent supporters of the Trans-Pacific Partnership (TPP), an extremely detrimental treaty that successfully surrenders American sovereignty to an international union consisting of 12 different countries, it is clear that Mrs. Clinton and our current president will not uphold the spirit in which our country was founded. It is also clear that the Globalists are circling the wagons around Hillary Clinton and they will do anything to protect her.

If Mrs. Clinton is elected as our 45th President, it will leave the door wide open to ratifying the TPP and our nation will no longer be sovereign; unable to enact or enforce our own laws.

We will become a borderless country, as Mrs. Clinton's immigration platform is the most radical in our history. She will expand President

Obama's agenda, throwing our immigration laws out the window by granting amnesty to millions of people here illegally, while releasing dangerous criminals back on our streets to live with our children and grandchildren through the Sentencing Reform and Corrections Act of 2015 (S. 2123).

There is only one sure way to stop this from happening and that is to elect Donald Trump as our next President. Hillary Clinton cannot be allowed to win.

Hillary Clinton's radical ideology will have devastating effects economically on the poorest of Americans, those whom she claims to champion. However, the African-American and Hispanic communities are consistently seeing a reduction in wages and the steady disappearance of jobs as they are snatched away by the huge influx of new foreign workers brought in by the Obama Administration.

This devastating cycle of poverty will only continue to grow if Hillary Clinton is elected.

Clinton's desire for a world without borders will be our countries undoing as it will allow untold millions more to flood our country. Americans are not a primary concern for either Mrs. Clinton or President Obama as their globalist views are rooted so deeply and nationalism, to them, is a racist and dirty word.

Republicans who are not firmly on the Trump bandwagon have persisted in saying that Mr. Trump is not a "real conservative" and that his views on such things as mass immigration from Middle Eastern countries, creating and enforcing fair trade and solving our countries border problems are not "who we are as Americans." But if you ask any hard-working American on the street, they will tell you that whether or not Mr. Trump is conservative or moderate is not the point.

What is the point, is that they believe that Donald Trump will restore our country to its former glory by taking a nationalist view and in doing so, he will indeed, with every decision he makes, restore our beloved country by making America First. That in my mind, and in the minds of Mr. Trump's supporters, is by definition, conservative.

Donald Trump and Hillary Clinton have very differing views on the role of government and they could not be more stark. As President, Donald Trump has maintained that after taking the oath, he would immediately repeal and replace Obamacare, place a halt on Obama's Executive Amnesty, begin building a wall on our southern border, and return power to the states. He will also rebuild our nation's roads and bridges as our infrastructure is crumbling beneath us.

He has maintained that his nomination for the vacant Supreme Court Justice seat would be a conservative justice, one who believes in our Constitution and the principals on which our country was founded.

Donald Trump will also replace Obama's radical Cabinet appointments, reduce corporate and small-business taxes and regulations which will allow for greater job creation and he will allow America to produce more of its own energy, reducing the strangle-hold that oil producing countries currently have on our economy. He will also rein in an out-of-control, power-hungry EPA and restore not only the coal mining industry but every other industry that Obama and the Democrats have sought to annihilate.

All these proposals by Donald Trump can do only one thing. They will restore America and allow us to be a Great Nation once again.

This election, the choice is simple: Do we want a country that serves our nation or do we want one that serves the globalist agenda, which will leave America and the American people behind forever? It seems like a clear choice for me. If we are going to leave our children a better and prosperous America, then we must take a Nationalist view at this point in our history.

Therefore we must elect the only man who will do that. We must take a stand now and vote America First, and that means electing Donald J. Trump as the 45th President of this country, because Mr. Trump is the only candidate who truly believes that America comes first.

With the amazing week Donald Trump has had it is reflecting in the polling. He is currently pulling ahead of Hillary Clinton nationally and hopefully he will continue the momentum.

We will all be there on election day to cast our vote for Donald Trump, because together we can Make America Great Again.

AFTERWORD

This was written by a young woman who wishes to remain anonymous so we will do her the honor and leave off her name. We will only call her a Patriot.

REASONS WHY I DO NOT SUPPORT DONALD TRUMP

"I do not support Donald Trump. I support me and mine. I do what I have to do and I do the best I can. So far so good."

"Somewhere along the way... I lost faith in what, as a child, I was taught America was all about. Holidays turned into hollow-days, especially on 4th of July, Memorial Day, Veterans Day, Flag Day and yes Christmas."

"With a tear in my eye and an ache in my heart I even re-wrote part of the National Anthem to "the land of the greed (Govt.) and the home of the slave (us)" and all I had .. all I HAVE is faith. I know as long as I believe in myself, and that what I'm doing is helping somebody, I can get through another day."

"Everything changed for me on June 16 2015. Donald J Trump officially announced his candidacy for President of The United States of America because he loves this country and wants to Make America Great Again."

"I do not support Donald Trump!"

"1. When he mentioned heroin coming across the border and he wants to stop it, he is supporting me.

2. When he says he wants to build a wall as a tool to help our Border Patrol keep our border secure, he is supporting me.

3. When he says he wants to clean up our sovereign nation by simplifying the immigration process so that all immigrants are quickly put onto the road to United States citizenship he is supporting me.

4. When he says he wants to ban any people that have brought terror into this country as a matter of religion and culture imitating freedom, when he wants to keep that out of the USA he is supporting me.

5. When he refuses to twist the truth and call it Political Correctness he supporting me.

6. When he defends our Second Amendment he is supporting me.

7. When he wants to repeal and replace a failed healthcare system he is supporting me.

8. When he supports our Vets he is supporting me.

9. When he wants to manufacture here again, he is supporting me.

I could go on and on... alright, one more.

10. When he blows the whistle on all the various forms of lies and corruption in the government and in the media, while taking incoming like the flag Francis Scott Key wrote about, I am one of those patriots keeping this movement going because he supports me."

"I don't support Donald Trump, I support me and mine. I do what I feel is best for me so I registered Republican, read The Art of the Deal, Crippled America is on my desk, voted Trump in the CA primary and on November 8 2016, I am going to support my country and vote Donald J. Trump for President of The United States of America; because he loves this country and by re-visiting and once again embracing the principles that our founding fathers fought and died for, together we can and will Make America Great Again."

To Patriots everywhere. God Speed!

Other books by Kimberly Bratton available on Amazon, CreateSpace and Smashwords

Donald Trump: An American Love-Fest

An in depth look at Trump supporters, who they are and what they want.

Donald Trump: The People's Choice

A complete look at the Trump campaign from the South Carolina debate and the death of Justice Antonin Scalia to the day he wins the nomination.

Holy Cow...I'm A Chicken Mama

A delightful, fun-filled book on my adventures as a Chicken Mama. Packed full of valuable information and fun stories. This has been my favorite book to write.

ENDNOTES

[1] https://en.wikipedia.org/wiki/United_Nations
[2] https://en.wikipedia.org/wiki/Dominant_ideology
[3] https://en.wikipedia.org/wiki/Globalism
[4] https://en.wikipedia.org/wiki/New_World_Order
[5] https://en.wikipedia.org/wiki/New_World_Order_(conspiracy_theory)
[6] https://en.wikipedia.org/wiki/Global_governance
[7] https://archive.org/details/anatomyofpeace009815mbp
[8] https://en.wikipedia.org/wiki/World_government
[9] http://www.breitbart.com/2016-presidential-race/2016/07/14/clinton-resettle-one-million-muslim-migrants-first-term-alone/
[10] This figure comes from the current data available from the Department of Homeland Security (DHS).
[11] http://www.breitbart.com/2016-presidential-race/2016/07/14/clinton-resettle-one-million-muslim-migrants-first-term-alone/
[12] http://www.breitbart.com/2016-presidential-race/2016/06/23/census-data-10-million-new-immigrants-enter-u-s-president-hillary-clintons-first-term/
[13] http://www.breitbart.com/2016-presidential-race/2016/05/26/ryan-launches-new-attack-trump-clinches-nomination/
[14] http://www.breitbart.com/2016-presidential-race/2016/07/14/clinton-resettle-one-million-muslim-migrants-first-term-alone/
[15] http://www.wsj.com/articles/the-rich-get-richer-as-billionaires-increase-in-number-1470628860
[16] http://www.atr.org/full-list-hillary-s-planned-tax-hikes
[17] http://www.hightaxhillary.com/
[18] Byron York, National Review, August 3, 2005: "Soros,

who would eventually give ACT $20 million of his own money..."

[19] "New Alliance of Democrats Spreads Funding." The Washington Post. Retrieved July 17, 2006.

[20] "Forbes 400 Richest Americans: George Soros." Forbes. September 2013. Retrieved November 19, 2013

[21] http://www.breitbart.com/london/2015/11/02/soros-admits-involvement-in-migrant-crisis-national-borders-are-the-obstacle/

[22] http://yournewswire.com/black-lives-matter-produced-by-george-soros/

[23] http://theglobalelite.org/globalists/#

[24] http://imgur.com/uud2syj

[25] http://www.goodreads.com/quotes/40800-world-events-do-not-occur-by-accident-they-are-made

[26] http://www.infowars.com/bilderberg-2016-to-talk-trump-riots-migrants-brexit/

[27] http://investmentwatchblog.com/david-rockefeller-some-even-believe-we-are-part-of-a-secret-cabal-working-against-the-best-interests-of-the-united-states-if-thats-the-charge-i-stand-guilty-and-i-am-proud-of-it-10-minu/

[28] http://www.illuminati-news.com/0/RussoRockefeller.htm

[29] http://www.breitbart.com/big-government/2015/04/26/11-explosive-clinton-cash-facts-mainstream-media-confirm-are-accurate/

[30] http://www.wnd.com/2015/05/here-they-are-hillarys-22-biggest-scandals-ever/

[31] http://www.realclearpolitics.com/epolls/other/direction_of_country-902.html

[32] https://www.youtube.com/watch?v=prXVUh47Obs

[33] http://www.infowars.com/burn-down-white-suburbs-sister-of-man-killed-by-milwaukee-police-urges-rioters/

[34] https://www.youtube.com/watch?v=NgNofUyM_Xw

[35] https://www.youtube.com/watch?v=IAjWtnGihYA

[36] https://www.youtube.com/watch?v=2BSV1jOQFKs